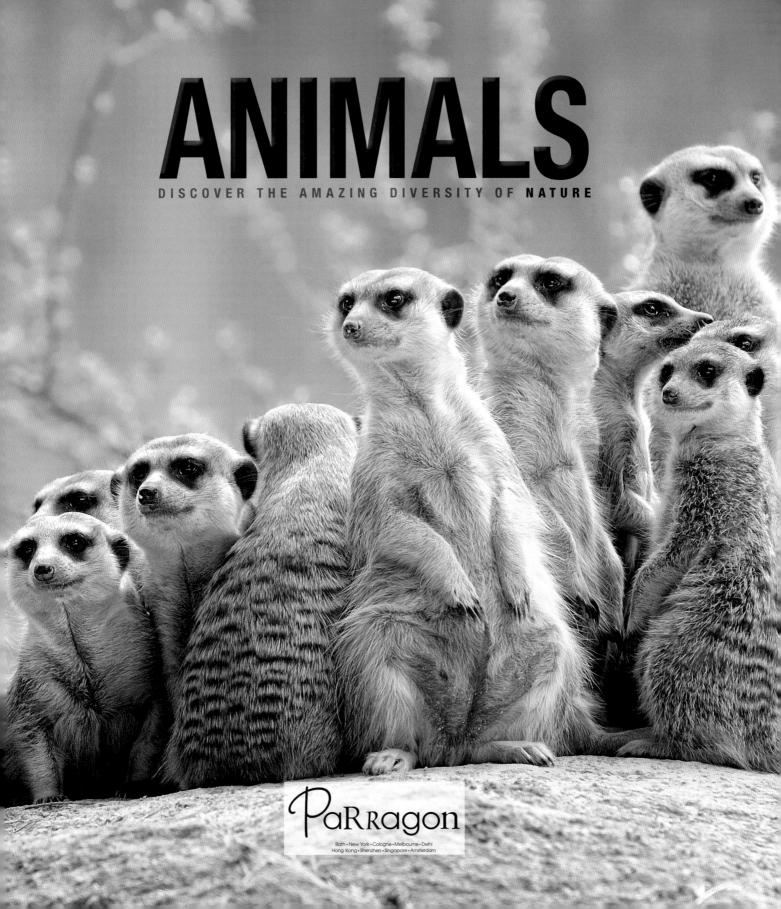

ANIMALS

DISCOVER THE AMAZING DIVERSITY OF NATURE

Discovery KIDS™

PaRragon

Bath · New York · Cologne · Melbourne · Delhi
Hong Kong · Shenzhen · Singapore · Amsterdam

This edition published by Parragon Books Ltd
in 2015 and distributed by

Parragon Inc.
440 Park Avenue South, 13th Floor
New York, NY 10016
www.parragon.com

This edition produced by Jollands Editions
Cover design by JC Lanaway

ISBN 978-1-4723-7674-9

Printed in China

Based on an idea by Editorial SOL 90

Cover images courtesy of istock

CONTENTS

INTRODUCTION	4
WHAT IS A MAMMAL?	8
LIFE CYCLES	10
DEVELOPED SENSES	12
SPEED AND AGILITY	14
MEAT EATERS	16
HERBIVORES	18
ONE FOR ALL	20
RECORD BREATH-HOLDERS	22
UNDERWATER LANGUAGE	24
NOCTURNAL FLIGHT	26
LIFE IN THE AIR	28
FEATHERS	30
FIRST, THE EGG	32
NO FLYING ALLOWED	34
FRESHWATER BIRDS	36
ARMED TO HUNT	38
THE PERCHERS CLUB	40
SKIN WITH SCALES	42
LIZARDS	44
VENERATED AND FEARED	46
DANGEROUS COILS	48
FISHY FEATURES	50
THE ART OF SWIMMING	52
DEADLY WEAPON	54
THE JOURNEY HOME	56
KINGS OF DARKNESS	58
BETWEEN LAND AND WATER	60
METAMORPHOSIS	62
JOINTLESS	64
COLORFUL ARMOR	66
EIGHT LEGS	68
SECRETS OF SUCCESS	70
THE ART OF FLYING	72
ORDER AND PROGRESS	74
SURVIVAL STRATEGIES	76
GLOSSARY	78
INDEX	80

INTRODUCTION

 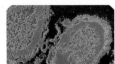 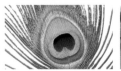   

Welcome to the amazing world of animals! In this fascinating book you can explore the astonishing lives of some of the millions of species with which we share the planet Earth.

Every region of our planet has been colonized by animals. As scientific understanding of the animal world increases, so does our appreciation of the intimate relationships between humans and other animal species, and of the need to conserve the rich diversity of life on Earth, for the sake of our own survival as well as theirs.

Animals are classified into five main groups: Mammals, Birds, Reptiles, Fish and Amphibians, and Invertebrates. Mammals are the smallest group, but they include the largest animal, the blue whale. Easily the biggest group, with myriads of individual animals in millions of species, are the Invertebrates.

Mammals

From the frozen tundra to the tropical rain forests, the Earth is rich in mammals, animals of astonishing diversity that have occupied a wide range of environments. Mammals probably began to dominate the Earth about 65 million years ago. Without a doubt, modern humans are the most successful mammals—we have explored and colonized all the Earth's habitats. Our domestic coexistence with other species began around 10,000 years ago, when human culture shifted from nomadic hunter-gatherers to a society based on agriculture. Humans began to domesticate some mammals for work, meat, and milk, and for useful products, such as wool and leather. These domestic animals included dogs, sheep, pigs, cows, goats, and horses.

There are 5,416 known mammal species. Their diversity is evident in their adaptation to different environments. Mammal species can run, glide, fly, jump, swim, and crawl. To survive the rigors of low temperatures, some cold-climate animals spend the winter in deep sleep to save energy. Most aquatic mammals have thick layers of body fat instead of hair, which in most land mammals serves to conserve heat. Seals, dolphins, bats, and chimpanzees all have upper limbs with

COMMUNICATION
The ways in which cetaceans communicate with others of their kind are among the most sophisticated in the animal kingdom. Dolphins, for example, click with their mandibles when in trouble and whistle repeatedly when afraid or excited.

similar bones, but seals have flippers, dolphins have fins, bats have wings, and chimpanzees have arms.

Birds

Birds never cease to amaze us. Avian abilities are varied, including diving, swimming, and complex nest-building skills, but their ability to fly has long been envied by humans. Many birds fly thousands of miles, crossing deserts and oceans to reach their breeding and feeding grounds. Much of bird behavior, such as the ability of migrants to find their way across continents and back, continues to be a mystery.

It is believed that there are approximately 9,700 bird species in the world. This makes birds the second largest vertebrate group of animals, after fish. Birds vary greatly in size: from a hummingbird weighing just $^3/_{50}$ ounce (1.6 g), to an ostrich weighing in at 330 pounds (150 kg). Although most birds fly, there are some flightless birds—such as kiwis, penguins, rheas, and ostriches. Other birds are adapted to aquatic life in oceans, rivers, and lakes. The shape of birds' feet and bills reflects adaptations. Some aquatic species have bills modified to filter feed on small particles in water, whereas birds of prey use hooked bills to hold down and tear apart prey. In many bird species, both males and females share nest making and the rearing of young, and some birds also display social behaviors in groups.

Reptiles

There are about 8,200 species of reptiles. They include turtles, lizards, snakes, and crocodiles. Reptiles were the first vertebrates to be independent of water. An amniotic egg with a waterproof shell enabled them to breed and hatch on land, without the need to return to water. Because reptiles rely on external heat to regulate their body temperature, many spend hours in sunlight, warming themselves by infrared radiation.

Humans have long feared and respected reptiles. Snakes, crocodiles, and mythical dragons are found in the legends of peoples throughout the world. Many reptile species have impressive abilities: they can scale walls, burrow, swim, climb slender stalks, and even run across loose, hot sand dunes. These amazing animals with extraordinary traits have been around for many millions of years. Today, however, many species of reptiles are in danger of extinction, threatened by hunting and destruction of their habitat.

Fish and Amphibians
Among the first vertebrates (creatures with internal skeletons) were fish and amphibians, and each species has evolved to help it survive in a specific habitat. Fish are uniquely adapted to the watery world, with gills for breathing and fins for swimming. They can live in oceans, lakes, and freshwater rivers and streams, while strange and little-known fish inhabit the cold, dark ocean depths. Many fish are valued as food by people, and the conservation of commercial fish stocks is a key issue for the future. Some fish remain elusive and even feared; few animals match the reputation in fact and fiction of the shark.

Way back in evolutionary prehistory, some species moved from water to dry land, breathing by means of lunglike air sacs. Fish with proto-limbs were able to exploit new food sources and, over time, adapted to life

GREEN TREE PYTHON
This tree-dwelling green python usually coils around a branch and waits with its head hanging down, ready to attack. It eats small mammals and birds.

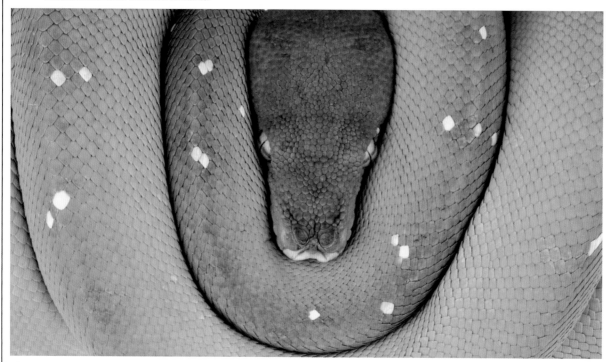

OWL
As a group, birds have exceptional eyesight—they have the largest eyes in relation to their bodies. This Cape eagle owl, *Bubo capensis*, is native to Africa. It feeds on birds and mammals.

on land. This evolutionary change—from water-dwelling to land-dwelling animals—constituted a revolution for life on Earth. Some land-dwelling animals retained a link with water through breeding behavior; these are the amphibians, such as frogs and toads. The living amphibians are a tiny fraction of a once-numerous class that appeared during the Devonian period of prehistory, but most became extinct during the later Triassic period.

Invertebrates
The most ancient forms of animal life on Earth are the invertebrates. They are also by far the most numerous. With more than 1.5 million known species, it is estimated that 97 percent of all animal species are invertebrates. This fascinating group of creatures offers amazing examples of adaptation and habits. Many invertebrates play a vital role in food chains and ecosystems, so they are very important to other species. Others are useful controls: without spiders as expert predators, the world might be overrun by insect pests.

Conserving the Natural World
We may wonder at the thousands of species of animals alive today. Yet it is thought that 99.9 percent of all the animal species that have ever existed are now extinct. Extinctions happen naturally, but human actions can also lead to species being lost forever. Modern science is showing us how all living things are interconnected in complex ecosystems. By learning more about animals, we will be better able to conserve the natural world and to protect the Earth's amazing wildlife for future generations.

What Is a Mammal?

Mammals share a series of characteristics that distinguish their class: a body covered by hair, the birth of live young, and the feeding of newborns on milk produced by the females' mammary glands. All breathe through lungs, and all possess a closed, double circulatory system and the most developed nervous systems in the animal kingdom. The ability to maintain a constant body temperature has allowed them to spread out and conquer every corner of Earth, from the coldest climates to hot deserts and from the mountains to the oceans.

GORILLA
Gorilla gorilla

A Body for Every Environment

Mammals have skin covered with hair and sweat glands, which helps create and maintain a constant body temperature. Eyes placed on each side of the head give monocular vision (except in the primates, which have binocular vision) but allow important angles of sight. The four limbs, ending in either feet or hands, vary in structure depending on the part of the foot used for walking. In aquatic mammals, the limbs have evolved into fins; in bats, into wings. Hunters are equipped with powerful claws, and unguligrades (such as horses) have strong hooves that support the whole body when running.

DISCOVERY FACT™

Gorillas share around 98 percent of their genetic makeup with humans, but chimpanzees are even closer relatives, with nearly 99 percent.

BOTTLENOSE DOLPHIN
Tursiops truncatus

Hair

Body hair is unique to mammals and absent in other classes of animals. Sirenians, with little hair, and cetaceans are exceptions; in both cases, the absence of hair is a result of the mammal's adaptation to an aquatic environment.

Teeth

Most mammals change their dentition in their passage to adulthood. Teeth are specialized for each function: molars for chewing, canines for tearing, and incisors for gnawing. In rodents, such as chipmunks, the teeth are renewed by continuous growth.

CHIPMUNK
Tamias sp.

Close Relatives

Humans belong to the primate group. The great apes (orangutans, gorillas, and chimpanzees) are the largest of our primate relatives, weighing between 105 and 595 pounds (48–270 kg). In general, males are larger than females, with robust bodies and well-developed arms. Like humans, their vertical posture differentiates their skeletons from those of other primates. Gorillas inhabit only the equatorial jungles of western Africa. They support themselves on their forelimbs while walking. Normally their height varies between 4 and 6 feet (1.2–1.8 m), but, if they raise their forelimbs and stand erect, they can be over 6½ feet (2 m) tall.

CRANIUM
Relatively large compared to the size of the body. And the brain is more developed and more complex than that of any other animal.

ALWAYS 98°F (37°C)
The ability to maintain a constant body temperature is not a characteristic unique to mammals: birds also have this ability.

AN EAR OF BONES
The tiny bones of the ear form a system for sensing and transmitting sound.

LOWER JAW
Formed by a single bone, called the "dentary," and teeth specialized for each function. The entire skull has a very simplified bone structure.

MAMMARY GLANDS
Secrete milk with which the females feed their young during their first months of life. These glands give the class its name.

A THICK SKIN
Formed by an outer layer (epidermis), another deeper layer (dermis), and a layer of fatty tissue that stores energy and helps regulate temperature.

Homeothermy

Mammals keep their body temperature relatively constant, independent of the ambient temperature. Hibernating species are the exception; they must lower their body temperature to enter this state of reduced metabolic activity. Contrary to popular belief, bears do not truly hibernate but rather enter into a period of deep sleep during winter.

GRIZZLY BEAR (BROWN BEAR)
Ursus arctos

Limbs

Mammals have four limbs that are adapted for moving about. The exceptions are the cetaceans, so adapted to marine life that their vestigial hind limbs are hidden inside their bodies. Forelimbs may have other abilities (such as seals' flippers for swimming, or hands for manipulation).

ELEPHANT SEAL
Mirounga sp.

5,416

IS THE NUMBER OF MAMMAL SPECIES ESTIMATED TO EXIST ON EARTH.

Take Habitat into Account

Between every mammal and its natural habitat there is a relationship that exists and is expressed in the animal's physical characteristics. Just as the flippers of the elephant seal are used to swim and hunt fish, mimicry and running are vital for deer. Physiology is a special instrument of adaptation to the environment, as in the case of the camel.

| Aquatic | Temperate forests | Desert | Meadow or pastureland |
| Tropical savanna | Tropical rain forest | Taiga | Tundra |

AN UNCOMMON PRIMATE

Humans have adapted to almost all habitats through their ability to modify certain elements of their habitat to their advantage. They often create tools to help them adapt to their environment. In this way, they do not need to rely on natural evolution alone. Humans have adapted to almost all habitats.

Life Cycles

Birth, maturity, reproduction, and death: this life cycle has certain particularities among mammals. As a general rule, the larger a mammal, the longer the members of its species tend to live but the fewer offspring are born to a single female per litter or reproductive season. Most mammals, including humans, are placental mammals; the young's vital functions are fully developed inside the body of the mother.

100 Years
IS THE AVERAGE LIFE SPAN OF A BOWHEAD WHALE—THE GREATEST OF ANY LIVING MAMMAL.

Placental Mammals

This is the largest group of mammals, the one that has multiplied most on the planet, although its form of gestation and lactation produces great wear and tear on females, making them less prolific. They are generally polygamous: a few males (the most competitive) fertilize many females, while other males have no offspring. Only 3 percent of mammals are monogamous in each season. In these cases, males participate in rearing young, as they also do when resources are scarce. If resources are abundant, the females take care of the young alone, and the males mate with other females.

They make use of natural caves or dig underground.

Weaning
35 TO 40 DAYS

Young rabbits remain with their mother even after nursing ends for protection and the inculcation of species-specific behavior.

Sexual Maturity
5 TO 7 MONTHS

The better rabbits are fed, the more quickly they become capable of reproducing. They are considered adults at 8 or 9 months, when they weigh around 2 pounds (900 g).

Lactation
25 TO 30 DAYS

The young are fed on milk, although they can digest solid food after 20 days. They abandon the burrow after 35 or 40 days but remain in the area where they were raised.

Females have four to five pairs of teats.

Female rabbits can mate at any time.

Longevity
4 to 10 years

Gestation
28 TO 33 DAYS

They spend it in a collective burrow (warren) dug in the ground and covered with vegetation and fur. The female will abandon the burrow as soon as lactation ends.

EASTERN COTTONTAIL RABBIT
Sylvilagus floridanus

4 inches (10 cm)

Rabbits are born without fur, with translucent skin.

AT BIRTH
The young weigh some $1^1/_2$ to $1^3/_4$ ounces (40–50 g). They do not open their eyes until the tenth day.

NUMBER OF OFFSPRING

In general, it is inversely proportional to the species' size.

COW	1 offspring
GOAT	2–3 offspring
DOG	5–7 offspring
RAT	6–12 offspring

3 to 9 young
PER LITTER, AND FROM 5 TO 7 LITTERS PER YEAR

Marsupials

After a very short gestation period, the young develop in a partially open pouch (called a "marsupium"), which the female carries on her belly. The majority of the roughly 300 known species of marsupials are solitary, except during mating periods. In general, they are promiscuous animals, although some, such as wallabies (small kangaroos), tend to mate with the same female throughout their life.

Lactation
22 WEEKS

A muscle inside the pouch prevents the infant from falling out. At 22 weeks, it opens its eyes, and a type of pap produced by its mother is added to its diet, which will prepare it for a herbivorous diet.

Gestation
35 DAYS

With its extremities and functional organs barely developed at birth, the newborn must crawl by itself from the cloaca to the pouch to continue its development.

The young animal fastens itself to its mother and is carried around by her, clinging to her shoulders.

BANISHED OFFSPRING
Dominant males keep the offspring and other young males apart.

Dominant males mate with all the females.

Some females leave to look for strong males.

KOALA
Phascolarctos cinereus

By the end of lactation, fur covers the whole body.

³/₄ inch (2 cm)

1 offspring
1 BIRTH PER YEAR

Leaving the Pouch
1 YEAR

The offspring reaches a size that allows it to fend for itself. It has already incorporated herbivorous food into its diet. The mother can become pregnant again, but the young will remain nearby.

Sexual Maturity
3 TO 4 YEARS

At two years, koalas already have developed sexual organs (females earlier than males). But they do not start mating until one or two years later.

Longevity
15 to 20 years

LONGEVITY

HUMANS	70 years
ELEPHANTS	70
HORSES	40
GIRAFFES	20
CATS	15
DOGS	15
HAMSTERS	3

GESTATION PERIODS

ANIMAL	MONTHS
Elephants	23
Giraffes	17
Gibbons	9
Lions	7
Dogs	2

COMPARISON OF EGG SIZE

The shell is soft and facilitates the offspring's birth. Unlike birds, they do not have beaks.

CHICKEN

ECHIDNA

Monotremes

Mammals whose females lay eggs are generally solitary species for most of the year. Platypuses are seen as couples only when they mate. Although they have a period of courtship for one to three months, the males have no relationship with the females after copulation or with the offspring. Short-beaked echidna females may be pursued by "trains" of up to ten males in the mating season.

Incubation
12 DAYS

Eggs gestate for a month before hatching. They incubate within a pouch for about ten days to remain at the proper temperature until the young are born.

Newborn offspring

Shell

½ inch (15 mm)

1 to 3
EGGS AT A TIME

In the Pouch
2 TO 3 MONTHS

After breaking the shell, the young are suckled while they remain in a pouch on the female's belly.

Undeveloped limbs

Underground cave or burrow among rocks

The fur is already spiny.

Weaning
4 TO 6 MONTHS

After three months, the offspring can leave the burrow or remain in it alone for up to a day and a half before finally separating from the mother.

Longevity
50 years

SHORT-BEAKED ECHIDNA
Tachyglossus aculeatus

Developed Senses

Dogs have inherited from wolves great hearing and an excellent sense of smell. Both perform an essential role in their relationship with their surroundings and their social activities. Whereas humans often remember other people as images, dogs do so with smell, their most important sense. They have 44 times more olfactory cells than humans, and they can discern one molecule out of a million others. They can hear sounds so quiet that they are imperceptible to people.

DISCOVERY FACT™

Dogs have at least 18 muscles that control the movements of their ears, allowing them to focus precisely on the source of a sound.

Hearing

The auditory ability of dogs is four times greater than that of human beings, and it is highly developed. Their ability depends on the shape and orientation of their ears, which allow them to locate and pay closer attention to sounds, although this varies by breed. They can hear sharper tones and much softer sounds, and they can directly locate the spatial reference point where a noise was produced. Dogs hear sounds of up to 40 kilohertz, whereas the upper limit for human hearing is 20 kilohertz.

INSIDE THE COCHLEA

Reissner's membrane
Scala vestibuli
Organ of Corti
Scala tympani

AURICULAR CARTILAGE

AUDITORY NERVE

LABYRINTH

SEMICIRCULAR CANALS

AUDITORY OSSICLES

INCUS (ANVIL)
MALLEUS (HAMMER)
STAPES (STIRRUP)

COCHLEAR NERVE

AUDITORY CANAL

MIDDLE EAR

COCHLEA

AUDITORY CANAL TYMPANIC MEMBRANE

Dome

INTERNAL STRUCTURE OF THE BULLA

Crest

Ciliary cells

The dome diverts sounds toward the bulla and other organs that direct electric signals to the brain.

OVAL WINDOW

EUSTACHIAN TUBE

COCHLEA

AUDITORY LEVELS

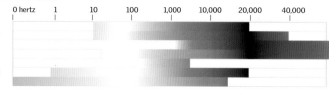

	0 hertz	1	10	100	1,000	10,000	20,000	40,000
HUMANS								
FOXES								
MICE								
BATS								
FROGS								
ELEPHANTS								
BIRDS								

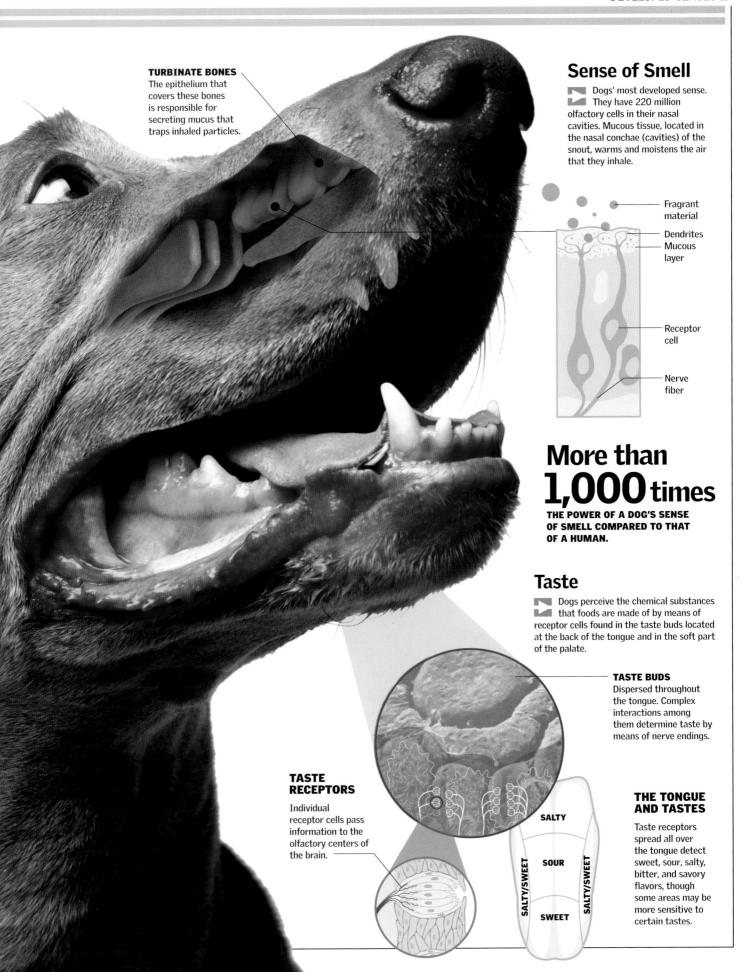

TURBINATE BONES
The epithelium that covers these bones is responsible for secreting mucus that traps inhaled particles.

Sense of Smell

Dogs' most developed sense. They have 220 million olfactory cells in their nasal cavities. Mucous tissue, located in the nasal conchae (cavities) of the snout, warms and moistens the air that they inhale.

Fragrant material

Dendrites

Mucous layer

Receptor cell

Nerve fiber

More than
1,000 times
THE POWER OF A DOG'S SENSE OF SMELL COMPARED TO THAT OF A HUMAN.

Taste

Dogs perceive the chemical substances that foods are made of by means of receptor cells found in the taste buds located at the back of the tongue and in the soft part of the palate.

TASTE BUDS
Dispersed throughout the tongue. Complex interactions among them determine taste by means of nerve endings.

TASTE RECEPTORS

Individual receptor cells pass information to the olfactory centers of the brain.

SALTY

SALTY/SWEET SOUR SALTY/SWEET

SWEET

THE TONGUE AND TASTES

Taste receptors spread all over the tongue detect sweet, sour, salty, bitter, and savory flavors, though some areas may be more sensitive to certain tastes.

Speed and Agility

They are meteors of flesh, bone, and hot blood. Cheetahs are members of the Felidae family and the fastest of all land animals, using their keen vision and great speed to hunt. They can reach 70 miles per hour (115 km/h) in short runs and accelerate to 45 miles per hour (72 km/h) in an average of only 2 seconds. They are also agile at high speed, making swift turns to catch their prey. They look like leopards, but their physical characteristics are different: they are built for speed, with long tails, slender bodies and limbs, and small, rounded heads.

TAKEOFF
From the top of a tree, the flying squirrel jumps toward another shorter tree.

Cheetahs

Whereas tigers prefer to lie in wait for prey and then jump on it, the cheetah uses explosive speed of more than 60 miles per hour (100 km/h) to run its prey down.

1 **Start**
The cheetah begins running by lengthening its stride and extending its four legs.

2 **Spinal Contraction**
Then it gathers its legs under its body, contracting its cervical spine to the maximum.

NOSTRILS
Very wide, they allow it to receive more oxygen as it runs.

ORDER	Carnivora
FAMILY	Felidae
SPECIES	Acinonyx jubatus (Africa)
	Acinonyx venaticus (Asia)

FIRST POINT OF CONTACT
As it runs, only one leg touches the ground at a time, but during the cervical contraction, the entire body lifts from the ground.

SECOND POINT OF CONTACT
Extending its four legs again, it picks up more momentum, supporting itself on only one back leg.

Bipeds versus Quadrupeds

18 MPH (29 KM/H)
SIX-LINED RACERUNNER
Cnemidophorus sexlineatus
Lizard endemic to the USA.

23 MPH (37 KM/H)
HUMAN BEING
Track record: Usain Bolt (Jamaica), 110 yards (100 m) in 9.58 seconds.

42 MPH (67 KM/H)
GREYHOUND
A dog with a light skeleton and aerodynamic anatomy.

50 MPH (80 KM/H)
HORSE
Anatomy designed for running, with powerful musculature.

70 MPH (115 KM/H)
CHEETAH
It only takes 2 seconds to reach a speed of 45 miles per hour (72 km/h).

IN THE AIR
The flying squirrel does not actually fly—it glides. Between its front and back limbs is a membrane of skin that, like a delta wing, stretches out the moment the animal jumps and stretches its legs. This allows it to glide from the top of one tree to the trunk of another.

Patagium

Tail acts like a rudder.

LANDING
While gliding, the squirrel can change its landing angle. Just before landing, it lowers its tail and raises its front legs, using the membrane like an air brake. It lands very gently on all four paws.

TOES
Upon landing, it grabs onto the surface with its toes.

Siberian Flying Squirrel

Flying squirrels (*Pteromys volans*) belong to the same rodent family as common squirrels, to which they are similar in both appearance and way of life. They live in the mixed forests of northern Europe, across Siberia, and into East Asia.

3 ## Extending the Spine

In a counterthrust opposing the contraction, the spine extends, creating forward momentum. The cheetah can cover 26 feet (8 m) in a single stride.

DISCOVERY FACT™

Cheetahs can't roar but are quite vocal: they communicate through chirping, churring, growling, hissing, and purring.

SHOULDER
The extensive flexion of the shoulder allows it to take very long leaps.

HEAD
Small and aerodynamic, with low air resistance.

TAIL
Large compared to the rest of the body, it acts as a pivot used to change direction suddenly.

LIMBS
Long and agile. It has a powerful, flexible skeleton and musculature.

70 miles per hour
(115 km/h)
MAXIMUM SPEED, BUT CAN BE MAINTAINED FOR ONLY 550 YARDS (500 M).

ZIGZAGGING AT HIGH SPEED

1 Cheetahs can make sharp turns while running at high speed.

2 These movements are possible because cheetahs grip the ground firmly with their claws.

PAWS

DIGITS
5 in forepaws
4 in hind paws

CLAWS
Unlike other felines, their claws are not fully retractable, allowing them to grip the ground better.

Sloth

These animals are notable for their extremely slow metabolism. They take half a minute to move a limb. They are also somewhat shortsighted, their hearing is mediocre, and their sense of smell barely serves to distinguish the plants on which they feed. They are the extreme opposite of cheetahs. However, since they live practically all their lives perched in trees, they do not need to move or see or hear precisely. They are perfectly adapted to their way of life.

THREE-TOED SLOTH
Native to the Amazon River basin.

Meat Eaters

The carnivore group is composed of species whose diet is based on hunting other animals. The kind of teeth they have help them efficiently cut and tear the flesh of their captured prey. Lions, the most sociable of the felines, have good vision and sharp hearing; they are the only cats to live in packs, and when they go hunting, they do so as a group.

Lions

are characterized by a strong, muscular physique. A male requires 15½ pounds of meat (7 kg) a day, whereas a female needs 11 pounds (5 kg). They have a short digestive tract, which rapidly absorbs nutrients from the meat they eat.

Teeth

UPPER PREMOLARS

UPPER INCISORS

UPPER CANINE

CARNASSIAL PAIR

They are very large, and the dental crowns are two long blades arranged as shears that fit into each other. Together they slice and cut flesh to perfection.

ANTERIOR PREMOLARS

LOWER CANINE

LOWER INCISORS

The Hunt

1 **LYING IN AMBUSH**
Hidden in the grass, the lioness silently approaches the prey. Other females wait in hiding.

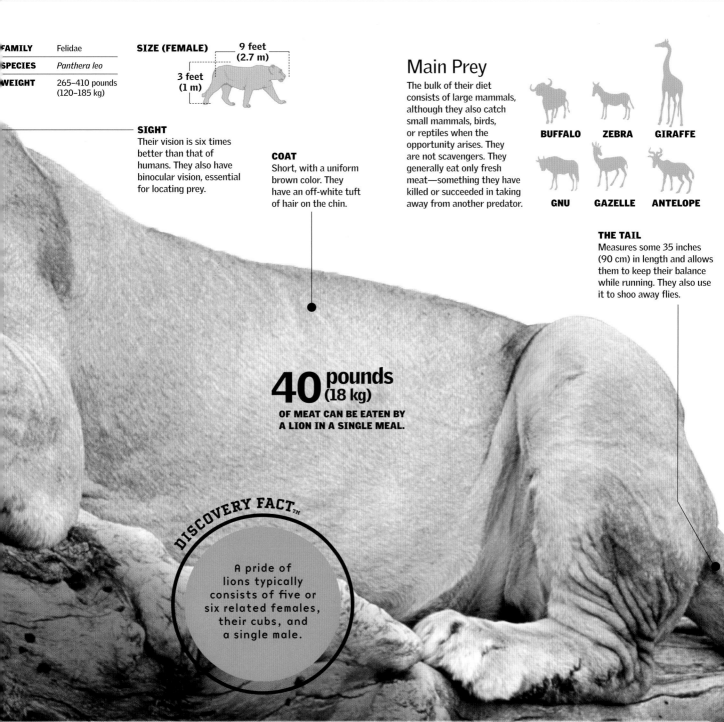

FAMILY	Felidae
SPECIES	*Panthera leo*
WEIGHT	265–410 pounds (120–185 kg)

SIZE (FEMALE)

9 feet (2.7 m)

3 feet (1 m)

SIGHT
Their vision is six times better than that of humans. They also have binocular vision, essential for locating prey.

COAT
Short, with a uniform brown color. They have an off-white tuft of hair on the chin.

Main Prey
The bulk of their diet consists of large mammals, although they also catch small mammals, birds, or reptiles when the opportunity arises. They are not scavengers. They generally eat only fresh meat—something they have killed or succeeded in taking away from another predator.

BUFFALO **ZEBRA** **GIRAFFE**

GNU **GAZELLE** **ANTELOPE**

THE TAIL
Measures some 35 inches (90 cm) in length and allows them to keep their balance while running. They also use it to shoo away flies.

40 **pounds (18 kg)**
OF MEAT CAN BE EATEN BY A LION IN A SINGLE MEAL.

DISCOVERY FACT™
A pride of lions typically consists of five or six related females, their cubs, and a single male.

2 **ACCELERATION**
When only a few yards away, the lioness starts running to catch the zebra. It exceeds 30 miles per hour (50 km/h), and the others cooperate in the hunt.

3 **LEAP**
The lioness hurls the weight of her body on the zebra's neck, trying to knock it down; if she succeeds, the hunt will be successful.

4 **LETHAL BITE**
The prey falls, and the lioness sinks her fangs into the neck until she kills it. The other females approach.

Herbivores

Ruminants, such as cows, sheep, and deer, have stomachs made up of four chambers with which they carry out a unique kind of digestion. Because these animals need to eat large quantities of grass very quickly in the wild—or else become easy targets for predators—they have developed a digestive system that allows them to swallow food, store it, and then return it to the mouth to chew calmly. When animals carry out this activity, they are said to ruminate, or chew the cud.

KEY

- ▰▰▰ INGESTION AND FERMENTATION
- ▰▰▰ RUMINATION
- ▰▰▰ REABSORPTION OF NUTRIENTS
- ▰▰▰ ACID DIGESTION
- ▰▰▰ DIGESTION AND ABSORPTION
- ▰▰▰ FERMENTATION AND DIGESTION

Teeth

Herbivorous animals, such as horses and cows, have molars with a large flat surface that reduces food to pulp, as well as incisors for cutting grass. Grinding is also done by the molars.

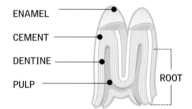

ENAMEL
CEMENT
DENTINE
PULP
ROOT

Cows wrap their tongues around the food.

Then they chew it with lateral movements.

1

Cows lightly chew grass and ingest it into their first two stomachs: the rumen and the reticulum. Food passes continually from the rumen to the reticulum (nearly once every minute). There various bacteria colonies begin fermenting the food.

2

When cows feel satiated, they regurgitate balls of food from the rumen and chew them again in the mouth. This is called rumination; it stimulates salivation, and, as digestion is a very slow process, cows make use of rumination to improve their own digestion together with the intervention of anaerobic microorganisms, such as protozoa, bacteria, and fungi.

40 gallons (150 L)

OF SALIVA ARE PRODUCED DAILY IN THE PROCESS.

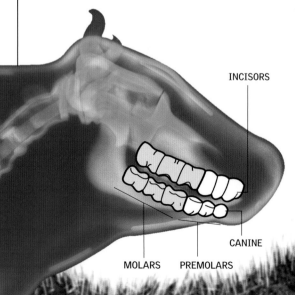

INCISORS

CANINE

MOLARS   PREMOLARS

THE RUMINATION PROCESS

helps ruminants reduce the size of the ingested food particles. It is part of the process that allows them to obtain energy from plant cell walls, also called fiber.

Ⓐ REGURGITATION   Ⓑ REMASTICATION   Ⓒ REINSALIVATION   Ⓓ REINGESTION

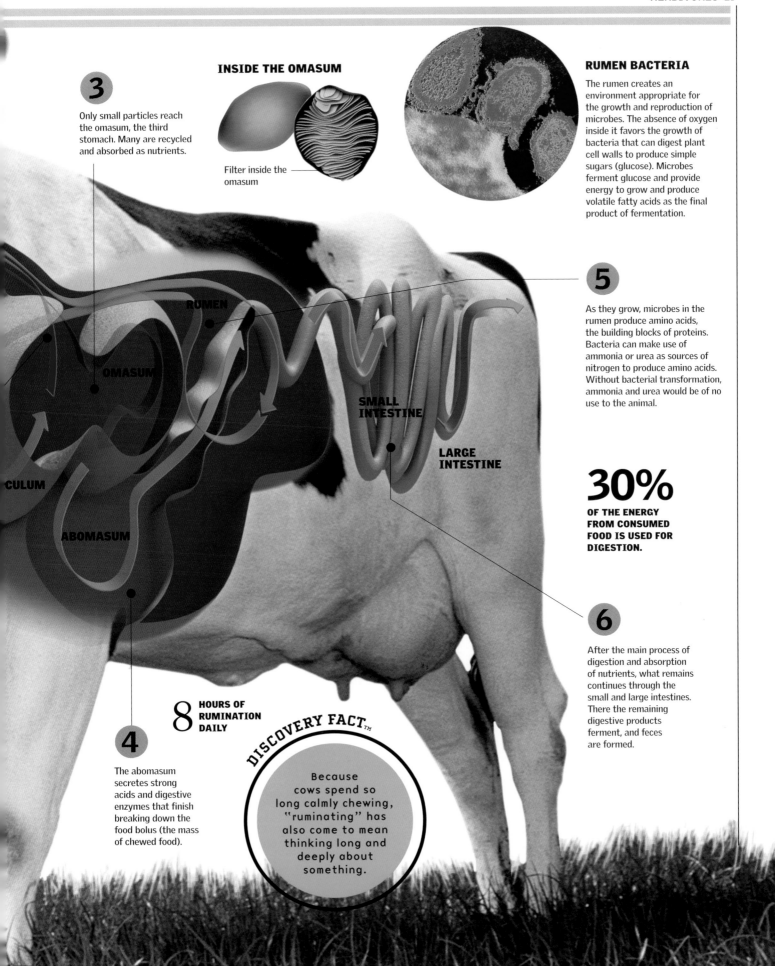

3

Only small particles reach the omasum, the third stomach. Many are recycled and absorbed as nutrients.

INSIDE THE OMASUM

Filter inside the omasum

RUMEN BACTERIA

The rumen creates an environment appropriate for the growth and reproduction of microbes. The absence of oxygen inside it favors the growth of bacteria that can digest plant cell walls to produce simple sugars (glucose). Microbes ferment glucose and provide energy to grow and produce volatile fatty acids as the final product of fermentation.

5

As they grow, microbes in the rumen produce amino acids, the building blocks of proteins. Bacteria can make use of ammonia or urea as sources of nitrogen to produce amino acids. Without bacterial transformation, ammonia and urea would be of no use to the animal.

RUMEN

OMASUM

SMALL INTESTINE

LARGE INTESTINE

CULUM

30%
OF THE ENERGY FROM CONSUMED FOOD IS USED FOR DIGESTION.

ABOMASUM

6

After the main process of digestion and absorption of nutrients, what remains continues through the small and large intestines. There the remaining digestive products ferment, and feces are formed.

8 HOURS OF RUMINATION DAILY

4

The abomasum secretes strong acids and digestive enzymes that finish breaking down the food bolus (the mass of chewed food).

DISCOVERY FACT™

Because cows spend so long calmly chewing, "ruminating" has also come to mean thinking long and deeply about something.

One for All

Meerkats are small mammals that live in underground colonies, posting guards while the mothers take care of their young. During the day, they go above ground to feed, and at night they go into the burrow to take refuge from the cold. In this large family, made up of dozens of members, each one fulfills a function. When faced with danger, they employ various tactics to defend themselves. One of these is the squeal that lookouts emit in the face of even slight dangers.

MEERKAT
Suricata suricatta

**12 inches
(30 cm)**

**Weight
2 pounds
(1 kg)**

FAMILY	Herpestidae
HABITAT	Africa
OFFSPRING	2 to 7

About
30 IS THE NUMBER OF
INDIVIDUALS A
GROUP CAN HAVE.

Social Structure

The social structure is extensive and well defined, ensuring that everyone has a role to fulfill. The lookouts (which may be female or male) take turns to sound the alarm over the arrival of strangers; one that is better fed replaces another that needs to eat. Meerkats are carnivorous: they eat small mammals, as well as insects and spiders.

FEMALES
must dedicate all their energy to the process of reproducing and feeding and raising young.

OFFSPRING
When the father or mother standing watch gives the cry of danger, all run to hide in the burrow.

BLACK-BACKED JACKAL
The meerkats' largest predator. To detect one before it is seen is of prime importance for the colony.

MARTIAL EAGLES
The most dangerous enemy they have and the one that kills the greatest number of meerkats.

Defense

1 SURROUNDING THE ENEMY
They emit a type of squeal. They rock back and forth. They try to appear larger and more ferocious than they are.

2 ON THEIR BACKS
If this tactic fails, they throw themselves down on their backs to protect their necks, showing their fangs and claws.

3 PROTECTION
When it is an aerial predator, they run to hide. If taken by surprise, adults protect the young.

Lookout

When a predator is detected, the lookout warns its group so that all of them can take cover in a nearby hole. This role rotates among different members of the group, and the warning is given by a very wide repertoire of sounds, each of which has a distinct meaning.

SIGHT
Binocular and in color, it allows them to locate their greatest predators, birds of prey.

HEAD
is kept permanently erect, observing the burrow's surroundings.

MALES
defend their territory and stand watch. The dominant male is the reproducer.

FRONT PAWS
They have strong claws, which they use for digging or to defend themselves.

MEERKATS ALSO USE VOCALIZATIONS TO COMMUNICATE.

VIGILANCE FROM ABOVE
It is common to see them at the highest spots of their territory, on rocks or tree branches.

DISCOVERY FACT™

Females without offspring act as babysitters for the young in the group while their mother is foraging for food.

Territory

The area defended provides the food necessary for the group's subsistence. Males devote themselves to defense, and when resources run out the group migrates to another area.

BURROWS
They dig them with their sharp claws and leave them only during the day.

HIND FEET
They support themselves on their hind feet when they remain standing, keeping watch.

TRIPOD TAIL
Meerkats use it to balance themselves when they are in an upright position.

Record Breath-Holders

Sperm whales are unique animals whose species is remarkable for many reasons. They have the ability to dive to a maximum depth of 10,000 feet (3,300 m) and remain underwater without oxygen for up to two hours. They are able to do this by means of a complex physiological mechanism that, for example, can decrease their heart rate, store and use air in the muscles, and prioritize the delivery of oxygen to certain vital organs, such as the heart and lungs. They are the largest whales to have teeth, which are found only on the lower jaw and fit into sockets in the upper jaw.

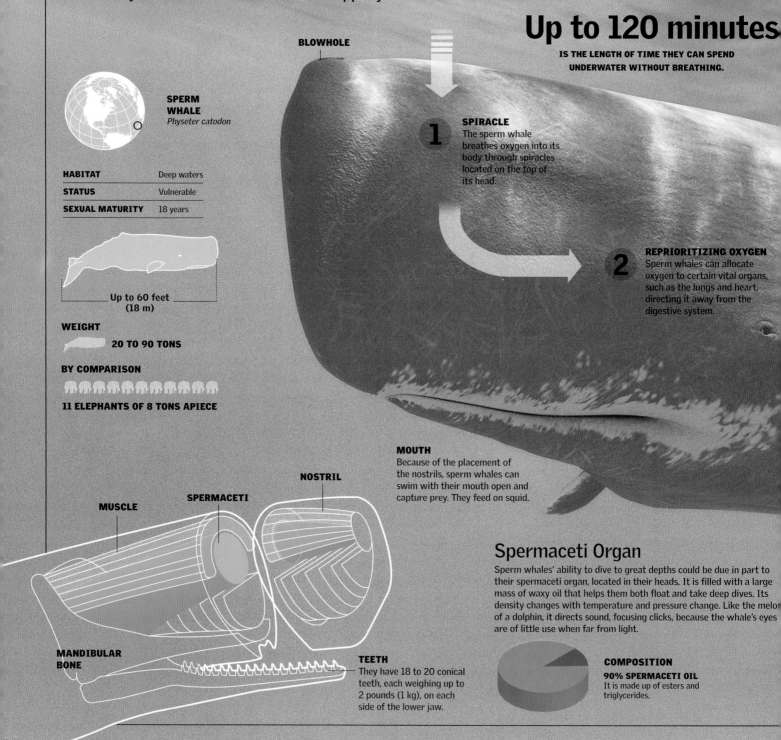

BLOWHOLE

Up to 120 minutes

IS THE LENGTH OF TIME THEY CAN SPEND UNDERWATER WITHOUT BREATHING.

SPERM WHALE
Physeter catodon

HABITAT	Deep waters
STATUS	Vulnerable
SEXUAL MATURITY	18 years

Up to 60 feet
(18 m)

WEIGHT

20 TO 90 TONS

BY COMPARISON

11 ELEPHANTS OF 8 TONS APIECE

1 SPIRACLE
The sperm whale breathes oxygen into its body through spiracles located on the top of its head.

2 REPRIORITIZING OXYGEN
Sperm whales can allocate oxygen to certain vital organs, such as the lungs and heart, directing it away from the digestive system.

MOUTH
Because of the placement of the nostrils, sperm whales can swim with their mouth open and capture prey. They feed on squid.

MUSCLE

SPERMACETI

NOSTRIL

MANDIBULAR BONE

TEETH
They have 18 to 20 conical teeth, each weighing up to 2 pounds (1 kg), on each side of the lower jaw.

Spermaceti Organ

Sperm whales' ability to dive to great depths could be due in part to their spermaceti organ, located in their heads. It is filled with a large mass of waxy oil that helps them both float and take deep dives. Its density changes with temperature and pressure change. Like the melon of a dolphin, it directs sound, focusing clicks, because the whale's eyes are of little use when far from light.

COMPOSITION
90% SPERMACETI OIL
It is made up of esters and triglycerides.

Adaptation in Respiration

When they dive to great depths, sperm whales activate an entire physiological mechanism that makes maximum use of their oxygen reserves. This produces what is called a thoracic and pulmonary collapse, causing air to pass from the lungs to the trachea, reducing the absorption of the toxin nitrogen. They also rapidly transmit nitrogen from the blood to the lungs at the end of the dive, thus reducing the circulation of blood to the muscles. Sperm whales' muscles contain a large amount of myoglobin, a protein that stores oxygen, allowing the whales to stay underwater much longer.

BLOWHOLE
Upon submerging, it fills with water, which cools the spermaceti oil and makes it denser.

HEART
The heart rate slows down during the dive, limiting oxygen consumption.

BLOOD
An ample blood flow, rich in hemoglobin, transports elevated levels of oxygen to the body and brain.

ON THE SURFACE
The blowhole remains open, allowing the whales to breathe as much oxygen as they can before diving.

WHEN THEY DIVE
Powerful muscles tightly close the opening of the blowhole, keeping water from entering.

RETIA MIRABILIA
The retia is a network of blood vessels (mirabilia) that filter the blood entering the brain.

LUNGS
absorb oxygen very efficiently.

TAIL
is large and horizontal and is the whale's main means of propulsion.

3 BRADYCARDIA
During a dive, the heart rate drops (a condition known as bradycardia), which lowers oxygen consumption.

DISCOVERY FACT™

From the eighteenth century, sperm whales were hunted for spermaceti oil, in demand for making candles, ointments, and cosmetics.

Dive

True diving champions, sperm whales can dive to depths of 10,000 feet (3,300 m), descending up to 10 feet (3 m) per second in search of squid. As a general rule, their dives last about 50 minutes, but they can remain underwater for up to two hours. Before beginning a deep dive, they lift their caudal (tail) fin completely out of the water. They do not have a dorsal fin, but they do have a few triangular humps on the posterior part of their body.

0 FEET (0 M)
ON THE SURFACE
They inhale oxygen through the blowhole located at the top of the head.

+ 3,300 FEET (1,000 M)
90 MINUTES
They store 90 percent of their oxygen in their muscles, so they can stay submerged for a long time.

0 FEET (0 M)
ON THE SURFACE
They exhale all the air from their lungs; this is called spouting, or blowing.

Making Use of Oxygen

Sperm whales can dive deeper and stay submerged longer than any other mammal, because they have various ways of saving oxygen: an ability to store it in their muscles, a metabolism that can function anaerobically, and the inducement of bradycardia during a dive.

15%
OF AIR REPLACED IN ONE BREATH

85%
OF AIR REPLACED IN ONE BREATH

Underwater Language

The ways in which cetaceans communicate with others of their kind are among the most sophisticated in the animal kingdom. Dolphins, for example, click when in trouble and whistle repeatedly when afraid or excited. During courtship and mating, they touch and caress each other. They also communicate through visual signals—such as leaping—to show that food is close by. They have a wide variety of ways to transmit important information.

HAVING FUN

Play for dolphins, as with other mammals, fulfills an essential role in the formation of social strata.

COMMON NAME	Bottlenose dolphin
FAMILY	Delphinidae
SPECIES	*Tursiops truncatus*
ADULT WEIGHT	330 to 1,400 pounds (150 to 650 kg)
LONGEVITY	30 to 40 years

7 to 13 feet (2–4 m)

THEY REACH 22 MPH (35 KM/H)

MELON

An organ filled with low-density lipids that concentrate and direct the pulses emitted, sending waves forward. The shape of the melon can be varied to better focus the sounds.

SPIRACLE   LIP

NASAL AIR SAC

DORSAL FIN
allows dolphins to maintain their equilibrium in the water.

CAUDAL FIN
has a horizontal axis (unlike that of fish), which serves to propel dolphins forward.

PECTORAL FIN

LARYNX

1 Emission

Sounds are generated by air passing through the respiratory chambers. But it is in the melon that resonance is generated and amplified. Greater frequencies and intensities are achieved in this way.

HOW THE SOUND IS PRODUCED

1 INHALATION
The spiracle opens so oxygen can enter.

SPIRACLE

Air to the lungs

2 The nasal air sacs begin to inflate.

They can go for 12 minutes without taking in oxygen.

4 The nasal air sacs deflate

Melon

SOUND

Air in the lungs

3 EXHALATION
Air resonates in the nasal sacs and the produced sound is directed through the melon.

Brain

MANDIBLE

The lower mandible plays a very important role in the transmission of sounds to the inner ear.

3 Reception and Interpretation

The middle ear sends the message to the brain. Dolphins hear frequencies from 100 hertz up to 150 kilohertz (the human ear can hear only up to 20 kilohertz). Low-frequency signals (whistles, snores, grunts, clicking) are key in the social life of dolphins, cetaceans that cannot live alone.

3 pounds
(1.4 kg)
HUMAN BRAIN

4 pounds
(1.7 kg)
DOLPHIN BRAIN

MORE NEURONS

A dolphin's brain, which processes the signals, has at least double the convolutions of those of humans, as well as nearly 50 percent more neurons.

MIDDLE EAR

2 Message

Low-frequency signals are used for communication with other dolphins, and high-frequency signals are used as sonar.

1 mile per second
(1.5 km/s)

SOUND WAVES TRAVEL 4.5 TIMES FASTER IN WATER THAN IN AIR.

DISCOVERY FACT

Cetacean mothers use echolocation while diving to keep track of their young calves, who need to stay nearer the surface to breathe.

Echolocation

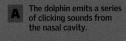

A The dolphin emits a series of clicking sounds from the nasal cavity.

B The melon concentrates the clicks and projects them forward.

C These waves bounce off objects they encounter in their way.

E The intensity, pitch, and return time of the echo indicate the size, position, and direction of the obstacle.

D Part of the signal bounces back and returns to the dolphin in the form of an echo.

SIGNAL WITH ECHO

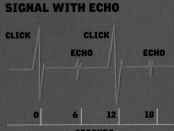

CLICK CLICK
ECHO ECHO

0   6   12   18
SECONDS

Nocturnal Flight

Bats are the only mammals that can fly. Scientists call them Chiroptera, a term derived from Greek words meaning "winged hands." Their forelimbs have been transformed into hands with very long fingers, joined together by a membrane (the patagium) that forms the surface of the wing. These mammals' senses are so sensitive that they can move and hunt quickly and accurately in the dark.

DISCOVERY FACT™

Bats are found all over the world, and they make up around 20 percent of all classified mammal species.

Expert Pilots

Moved by their chest and back muscles, bats' wings push downward and backward, generating both thrust and lift. Then the wings spread sideways and upward. Finally, they move forward until the tips almost rub the bat's head. Many of these flying mammals can drift through the air, gliding without flapping and maneuvering by folding their wings.

Their Radar

Most of the time bats fly at night in near-total darkness. Instead of light, they use a natural system similar to sonar or radar to guide themselves. This system uses acoustical signals the bats themselves emit while flying. This system allows them to recognize the location of any object in front of them or of prey, along with its direction, size, or speed. It is as if they were seeing without light.

1 The animal emits an acoustical vibration imperceptible to the human ear because of its high frequency (up to 80 kilohertz). The signal strikes the objects around it.

2 When the signals bounce back, the bat perceives their intensity and phase difference—the faster and more intense the return signal, the nearer the object or prey.

60 miles per hour
(97 km) IS THE SPEED SOME BATS MAY REACH DURING FLIGHT.

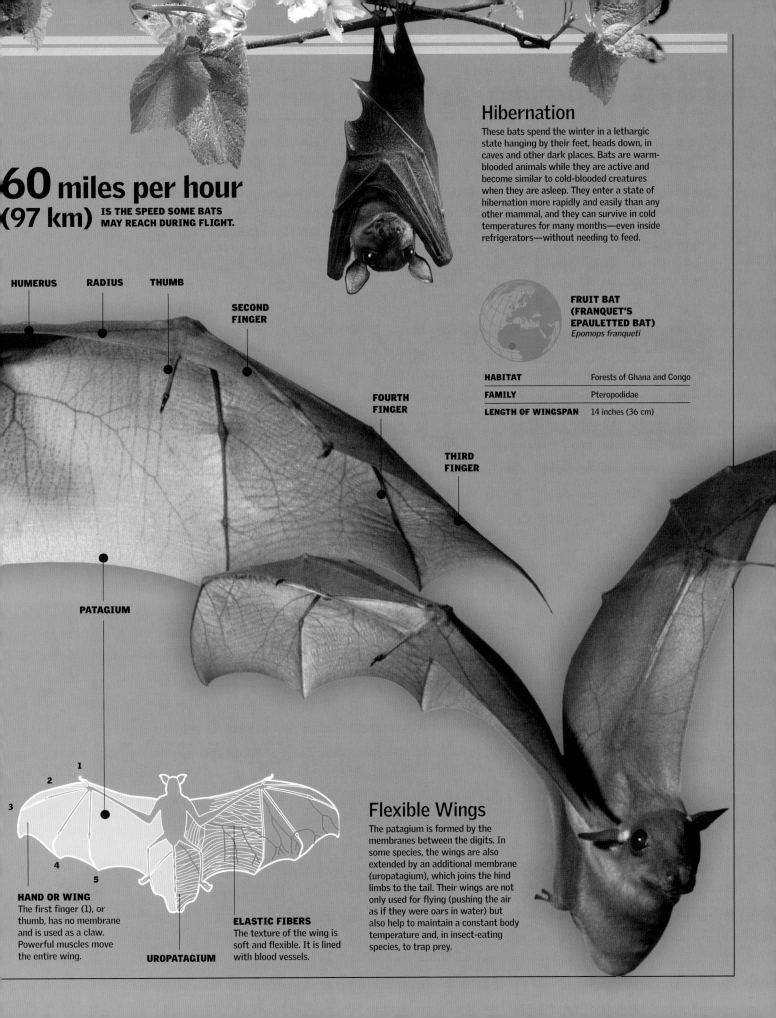

Hibernation

These bats spend the winter in a lethargic state hanging by their feet, heads down, in caves and other dark places. Bats are warm-blooded animals while they are active and become similar to cold-blooded creatures when they are asleep. They enter a state of hibernation more rapidly and easily than any other mammal, and they can survive in cold temperatures for many months—even inside refrigerators—without needing to feed.

FRUIT BAT (FRANQUET'S EPAULETTED BAT)
Epomops franqueti

HABITAT	Forests of Ghana and Congo
FAMILY	Pteropodidae
LENGTH OF WINGSPAN	14 inches (36 cm)

HUMERUS

RADIUS

THUMB

SECOND FINGER

FOURTH FINGER

THIRD FINGER

PATAGIUM

Flexible Wings

The patagium is formed by the membranes between the digits. In some species, the wings are also extended by an additional membrane (uropatagium), which joins the hind limbs to the tail. Their wings are not only used for flying (pushing the air as if they were oars in water) but also help to maintain a constant body temperature and, in insect-eating species, to trap prey.

HAND OR WING
The first finger (1), or thumb, has no membrane and is used as a claw. Powerful muscles move the entire wing.

UROPATAGIUM

ELASTIC FIBERS
The texture of the wing is soft and flexible. It is lined with blood vessels.

Life in the Air

Both lightweight and resistant, the skeleton of birds underwent important changes in order to adapt to flight. Some bones, like those of the skull and wings, fused to become lighter. Birds have fewer bones than other vertebrates. Because their bones are hollow, containing internal air chambers, the total weight of their skeleton is less than that of their feathers. Birds' spines tend to be very flexible in the cervical region and rigid near the rib cage, which joins a large, curved frontal bone called the "sternum." The sternum features a large keel, to which the pectoral muscles attach. These large, strong muscles are used for flapping the wings. In contrast, running birds, such as ostriches, have more developed muscles in their legs.

EYE SO

Flapping Wings

Flying demands an enormous amount of energy and strength. Consequently, the muscles responsible for flapping the wings become very large, easily comprising 15 percent of the weight of a flying bird. Two pairs of pectorals, in which one muscle of the pair is bigger than the other, work to raise and lower the wings. They function symmetrically and in opposition to each other: when one contracts, the other relaxes. Their placement within the thoracic cavity corresponds roughly to the bird's center of gravity. The motion of the wings also requires strong tendons.

HUMMINGBIRD
Because of its adaptation to stationary flight, its pectoral muscles account for as much as 40 percent of its total weight.

SKULL
Light because of the fusing of bones, the skull does not have teeth, a bony jaw, or grinding muscles.

UPPER MANDIBLE OF BILL
In some species, it is flexible.

LOWER MANDIBLE OF BILL
It is flexible, allowing birds to open their mouths wide.

FURCULA (COLLARBONE)
Also known as the wishbone, it is unique to birds and results from the fusion of the collarbones.

STERNUM
Hyperdeveloped in flying birds, the sternum's long keel facilitates the attachment of the pectorals.

WINGS

Without doubt, wings are the greatest adaptation of birds. Strong tendons travel through the wings and merge into the hand bones, where the feathers are attached.

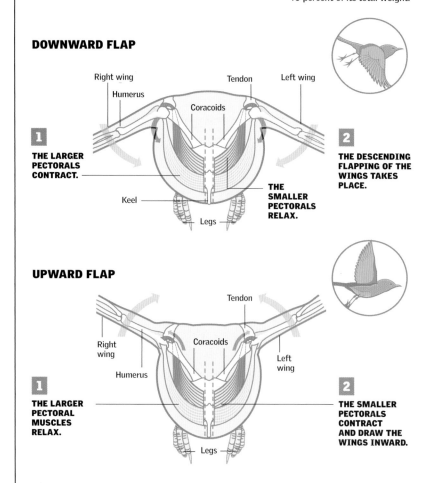

DOWNWARD FLAP

Right wing
Humerus
Tendon
Left wing
Coracoids

1
THE LARGER PECTORALS CONTRACT.

Keel
Legs

2
THE DESCENDING FLAPPING OF THE WINGS TAKES PLACE.

THE SMALLER PECTORALS RELAX.

UPWARD FLAP

Tendon
Right wing
Coracoids
Left wing
Humerus

1
THE LARGER PECTORAL MUSCLES RELAX.

Legs

2
THE SMALLER PECTORALS CONTRACT AND DRAW THE WINGS INWARD.

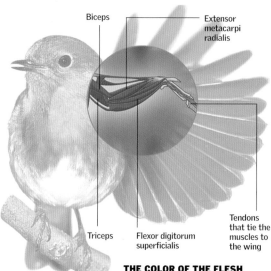

Biceps
Extensor metacarpi radialis

Triceps
Flexor digitorum superficialis
Tendons that tie the muscles to the wing

THE COLOR OF THE FLESH
depends on the blood circulation in the muscles: the more circulation, the redder the flesh. Flying birds have red flesh, while nonflying birds, such as chickens, have white flesh.

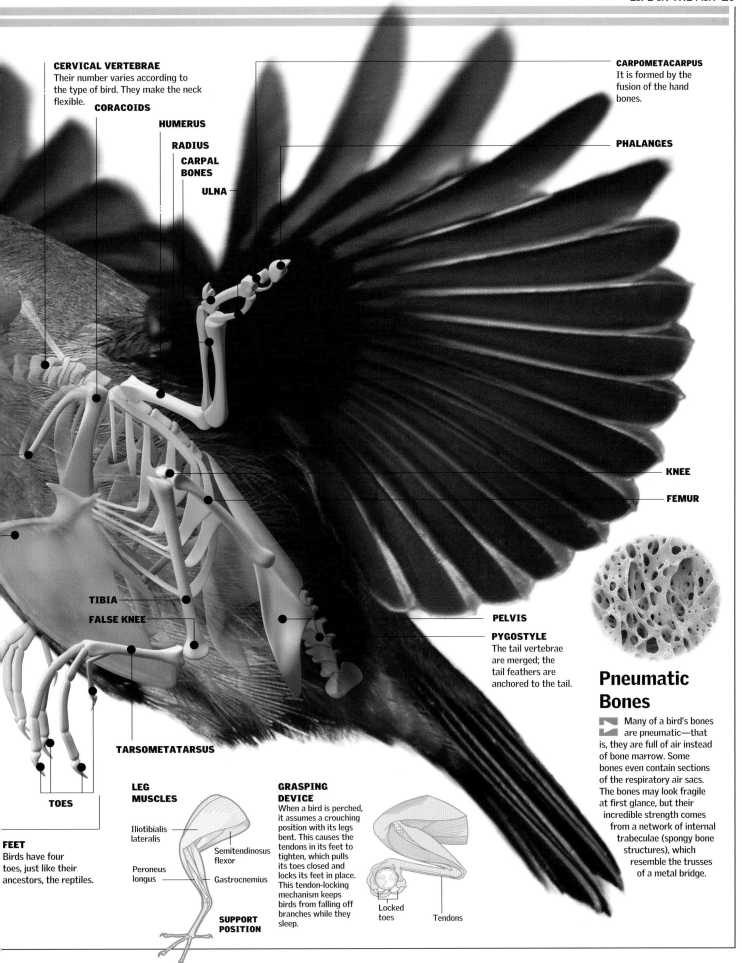

CERVICAL VERTEBRAE
Their number varies according to the type of bird. They make the neck flexible.

CORACOIDS

HUMERUS

RADIUS

CARPAL BONES

ULNA

CARPOMETACARPUS
It is formed by the fusion of the hand bones.

PHALANGES

KNEE

FEMUR

TIBIA

FALSE KNEE

TARSOMETATARSUS

TOES

PELVIS

PYGOSTYLE
The tail vertebrae are merged; the tail feathers are anchored to the tail.

FEET
Birds have four toes, just like their ancestors, the reptiles.

LEG MUSCLES

Iliotibialis lateralis

Semitendinosus flexor

Peroneus longus

Gastrocnemius

SUPPORT POSITION

GRASPING DEVICE
When a bird is perched, it assumes a crouching position with its legs bent. This causes the tendons in its feet to tighten, which pulls its toes closed and locks its feet in place. This tendon-locking mechanism keeps birds from falling off branches while they sleep.

Locked toes

Tendons

Pneumatic Bones

Many of a bird's bones are pneumatic—that is, they are full of air instead of bone marrow. Some bones even contain sections of the respiratory air sacs. The bones may look fragile at first glance, but their incredible strength comes from a network of internal trabeculae (spongy bone structures), which resemble the trusses of a metal bridge.

Feathers

Feathers are the feature that distinguishes birds from all other animals. They make birds strikingly colorful, protect them against cold and intense heat, enable them to move easily through the air and water, and hide them from enemies. Feathers are also one of the reasons why human beings have domesticated, caught, and hunted birds. A bird's set of feathers is called its "plumage," and its color is essential for reproductive success.

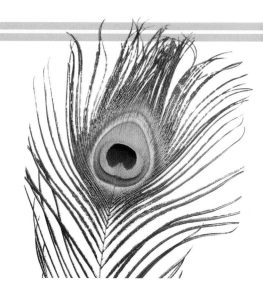

Structure

The structure of feathers has two parts: a shaft and a blade. The shaft is called the rachis, and the part connected to the bird's skin is called the calamus, or quill. The movement of a feather is generated in the rachis. The blade is composed of barbs that branch into barbules. The feather's blade, in which the barbules have a series of barbicels, or hooklets, at the tip, is called a vane. The interlocking hooklets in the vane create a network that adds rigidity and resistance to the feather. It also defines the characteristic aerodynamic shape of feathers and helps make the feather waterproof. When feathers wear out, birds have the ability to replace them with new ones.

1 A swelling, or papilla, develops in the bird's skin.

2 In the papilla, special skin cells form a follicle.

3 A tube that will extend from its base and become a feather grows in the follicle.

RACHIS
A feather's main shaft, similar to a hollow rod

EDGE
The edge presents an excellent aerodynamic profile for flying.

INFERIOR UMBILICUS
The orifice at the base of the calamus, into which the dermic papilla penetrates. New feathers receive nourishment through it.

HOLLOW INTERIOR

INNER PULP OF THE SHAFT

CALAMUS
It provides the necessary nutrients for feathers to grow. Nerve endings that stimulate the feather's movement are found at its base. This allows the bird to detect changes in its surroundings.

SUPERIOR UMBILICUS
It contains some loose barbs. Some feathers have a secondary rachis, the hyporachis.

BARBS
are slim, straight ramifications that grow perpendicular to the rachis.

Types of Feathers

There are three main types of feathers, classified according to placement: those closest to the body are down, or underlying feathers; those at the top are contour feathers; and those on the wings and tail are flight feathers, often referred to as remiges (on the wings) and rectrices (on the tail).

DOWN
These light and silky feathers protect the bird against the cold. They have a short rachis, or none at all. Their barbs are long, and their barbules lack hooklets. In general, down is the first type of feather that birds develop when they hatch.

CONTOUR
Also called covert feathers, they are short and rounded. They are more rigid than down feathers. Because they cover the body, wings, and tail, they give birds their shape as they fly.

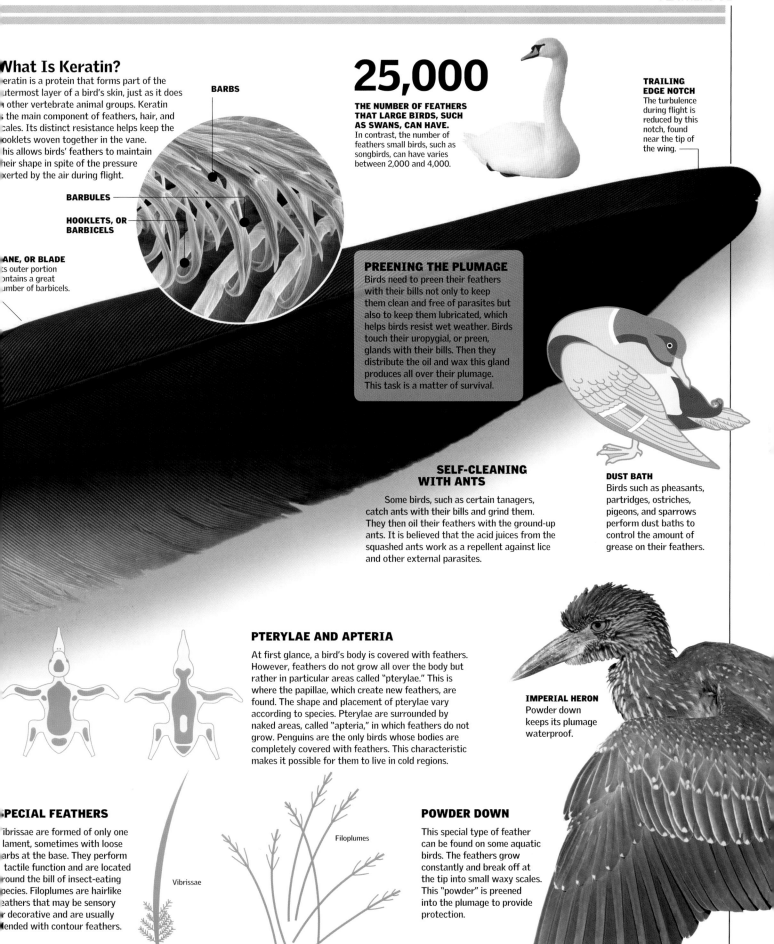

What Is Keratin?

Keratin is a protein that forms part of the outermost layer of a bird's skin, just as it does in other vertebrate animal groups. Keratin is the main component of feathers, hair, and scales. Its distinct resistance helps keep the hooklets woven together in the vane. This allows birds' feathers to maintain their shape in spite of the pressure exerted by the air during flight.

BARBS

BARBULES

HOOKLETS, OR BARBICELS

VANE, OR BLADE
Its outer portion contains a great number of barbicels.

25,000

THE NUMBER OF FEATHERS THAT LARGE BIRDS, SUCH AS SWANS, CAN HAVE.
In contrast, the number of feathers small birds, such as songbirds, can have varies between 2,000 and 4,000.

TRAILING EDGE NOTCH
The turbulence during flight is reduced by this notch, found near the tip of the wing.

PREENING THE PLUMAGE
Birds need to preen their feathers with their bills not only to keep them clean and free of parasites but also to keep them lubricated, which helps birds resist wet weather. Birds touch their uropygial, or preen, glands with their bills. Then they distribute the oil and wax this gland produces all over their plumage. This task is a matter of survival.

SELF-CLEANING WITH ANTS
Some birds, such as certain tanagers, catch ants with their bills and grind them. They then oil their feathers with the ground-up ants. It is believed that the acid juices from the squashed ants work as a repellent against lice and other external parasites.

DUST BATH
Birds such as pheasants, partridges, ostriches, pigeons, and sparrows perform dust baths to control the amount of grease on their feathers.

PTERYLAE AND APTERIA
At first glance, a bird's body is covered with feathers. However, feathers do not grow all over the body but rather in particular areas called "pterylae." This is where the papillae, which create new feathers, are found. The shape and placement of pterylae vary according to species. Pterylae are surrounded by naked areas, called "apteria," in which feathers do not grow. Penguins are the only birds whose bodies are completely covered with feathers. This characteristic makes it possible for them to live in cold regions.

IMPERIAL HERON
Powder down keeps its plumage waterproof.

SPECIAL FEATHERS
Vibrissae are formed of only one filament, sometimes with loose barbs at the base. They perform a tactile function and are located around the bill of insect-eating species. Filoplumes are hairlike feathers that may be sensory or decorative and are usually blended with contour feathers.

Vibrissae

Filoplumes

POWDER DOWN
This special type of feather can be found on some aquatic birds. The feathers grow constantly and break off at the tip into small waxy scales. This "powder" is preened into the plumage to provide protection.

First, the Egg

Birds may have inherited their reproductive method from their predecessors, the theropod reptiles. In general, they lay as many eggs as they can care for until the chicks become independent. Highly adapted to the environment, the eggs of the same species have varying shapes and colors. These variations help keep them safe from predators. They also vary greatly in size: the egg of an ostrich is 2,000 times bigger than that of a hummingbird.

How It Forms

Birds have only one functional ovary, the left one, which grows dramatically during the mating season. The ovule can descend and form what are known as unfertilized eggs (the type used in cooking). If the egg is fertilized, embryonic development begins. The ovule, fertilized or not, descends to the cloaca in a few hours or days. The eggshell begins to be formed at the isthmus, through the secretion of calcium. At first soft, the shell hardens when it comes in contact with the air.

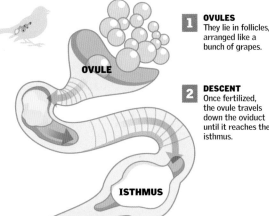

OVULE

ISTHMUS

CLOACA

1 OVULES
They lie in follicles, arranged like a bunch of grapes.

2 DESCENT
Once fertilized, the ovule travels down the oviduct until it reaches the isthmus.

3 SHELL
In the isthmus, the shell membranes form.

5 CLOACA
It expels the egg 24 hours later on average (in chickens).

4 UTERUS
The egg becomes pigmented, and the shell hardens.

CLUTCH

A group of eggs laid at one time is called a "clutch." During the mating season, a sparrow can have several clutches. If some eggs are removed, the sparrow can replace them without difficulty.

 2

As it feeds to grow, the embryo produces waste that is kept in a special sac.

 WASTE SAC

CHORION
protects and contains the embryo and its food.

YOLK

YOLK SAC

ALBUMEN

 1

The egg contains an embryo in one side of the yolk. The yolk is held in the middle of the white (albumen) by two protein cords, isolating it from the outside world.

EMBRYO

PROTEIN CORD (CHALAZA)

 3

Most birds' organs are formed in the first hours of incubation.

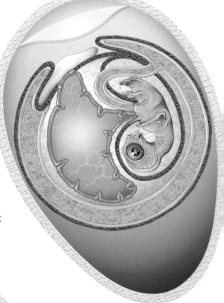

SHAPE

It depends on the pressure exerted by the oviduct walls. The large end emerges first.

Oval: The most frequent

Conical: Prevents falling

Spherical: Reduces the surface area

COLOR AND TEXTURE

Both texture and color help parents locate their eggs.

 Light Egg

 Dark Egg

 Speckled Egg

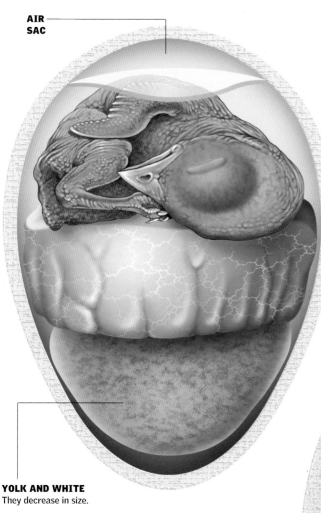

AIR SAC

YOLK AND WHITE
They decrease in size.

4

The bill and scales of the legs harden toward the end, when the chick is formed and reaches a size similar to that of the egg. At that point, rotation begins so that the chick will be positioned to break its shell.

5

By the time the chick is ready to break the shell, it is taking up all the space inside the egg. The chick is cramped with its legs against its chest. This enables it to open the shell with small movements and with the help of a hard point at the tip of its bill, called an "egg tooth."

SIZE

There is no exact proportion between the size of a bird and its egg.

1 pound (500 g)
KIWI'S EGG

2 ounces (60 g)
CHICKEN'S EGG

THE SHELL

Formed by a solid layer of calcium carbonate (calcite), it has pores that enable the chick to breathe. Bacteria are kept out by two semipermeable membranes that line the shell.

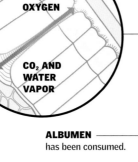

PORE **SHELL** **OUTER AND INNER MEMBRANES**

OXYGEN

CO_2 AND WATER VAPOR

8%

IS THE PROPORTION OF AN EGG TAKEN UP BY THE EGGSHELL.

ALBUMEN
has been consumed.

YOLK
disappears into the body.

No Flying Allowed

A few birds have lost their ability to fly. Their main characteristic is wing loss or reduction, although for some a remarkable size may be the cause of their inability to fly. Such birds weigh more than 39 pounds (18 kg). This is the case with runners (ostriches, cassowaries, emus, rheas, kiwis); extremely fast birds that live in remote areas of New Zealand; and swimmers, such as penguins, that have developed extraordinary aquatic abilities.

AFRICAN OSTRICH
A single species inhabits eastern and southern Africa. Adults reach a height of 9 feet (2.75 m) and a weight of 330 pounds (150 kg).

Super Swimmers

Penguins' bodies are covered with three layers of small, overlapping feathers. A penguin has small limbs and a hydrodynamic shape that helps it swim with agility and speed. Dense, waterproof plumage and a layer of fat insulate the bird from the low temperatures of the regions where it lives. Because its bones are rigid and compact, it is able to submerge itself easily. This adaptation distinguishes it from flying birds, whose bones are light and hollow.

DISCOVERY FACT™

The dodo was a flightless bird endemic to Mauritius that was hunted to extinction by sailors in the seventeenth century.

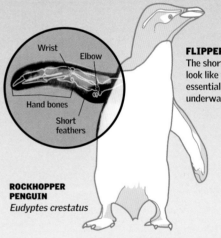

Wrist
Elbow
Hand bones
Short feathers

FLIPPERS
The short, compact wings look like flippers. They are essential to the penguin's underwater movements.

ROCKHOPPER PENGUIN
Eudyptes crestatus

SMALL HEAD

LONG NECK

ATROPHIED WINGS

PELVIS

FLAT STERNUM

ROBUST BONE

PENGUIN HEADING TO THE WATER

HUNTING
The wings work like flippers. The foot—with four joined toes pointing backward—and the tail steer the direction of the dive.

BREATHING
When looking for food, penguins need to leave the water and take a breath between plunges.

RELAXING
When resting in the water, they move slowly. They float on the surface with their heads up and balance their bodies with their wings and feet.

RUNNER'S CHEST

The keel-shaped sternum of flying and swimming birds offers a larger surface for attachment of the pectoral muscles. The flat sternum of running birds has a smaller surface and, consequently, less mobility.

KEEL-SHAPED STERNUM

The Ratites

Running birds belong to the group of the ratites (*rata* = raft, an allusion to the flat sternum). The forelimbs are either atrophied or have functions unrelated to flying. The hind limbs have very strong muscles as well as sturdy, vigorous bones. Another difference is found in the sternum. It is a flat bone without a keel, which flying and swimming birds possess. Wild ratites can be found only in the Southern Hemisphere. The Tinamidae, native to Central and South America, belong to this group (partridges).

6 feet (1.8 m)

4 feet (1.2 m)

4¹/₂ feet (1.4 m)

1¹/₄ feet (0.4 m)

STRUTHIONIFORMES
The ostrich is the only species in this group. It uses its wings for balance when running fast. It has only two toes on each foot. The adult male can weigh up to 330 pounds (150 kg).

RHEIFORMES
Rheas are common in South American countries, such as Argentina. They look like ostriches but are smaller. Their three-toed feet allow them to chase prey. Their long necks and excellent eyesight make them skillful hunters.

CASUARIIFORMES
Agile runners and swimmers. The colors on their necks and heads are distinctive. A bony hoof protects them from vegetation when they run. They have long, sharp talons on their feet.

APTERYGIFORMES
Kiwis. These birds have four toes on each foot, and their feathers look like fur because they do not have barbules. They use their keen sense of smell to find insects, usually at night. They lay only one large egg.

MAORI HEN
Gallirallus australis

ASIA

OCEANIA

AUSTRALIA

NEW ZEALAND

2 feet (0.6 m)

Running and Kicking

Ostriches usually run to escape from predators or to hunt small lizards and rodents. In both cases, because of their strong legs, they are able to reach a speed of 45 miles per hour (72 km/h) and to maintain it for 20 minutes. When running is not enough to protect the bird, it may resort to kicking to discourage its attacker. In courtship displays, forceful stamping is also used to win over females.

GREATER DIVERSITY
Running birds can be found in many parts of the world, largely because of human intervention. The area where flightless birds have diversified the most is Oceania (including Australia, New Zealand, and Papua New Guinea), due to continental isolation.

18
VERTEBRAE IN THE NECK OF AN OSTRICH.

TARSUS METATARSUS

PHALANGEAL CUSHION

PHALANGES

TOE

CLAW

PLANTAR CUSHION

ON TWO TOES
With just two toes, the contact surface between the foot and the ground is relatively small. This is an advantage when moving on land.

Other Walkers

More than 260 species belong to the order Galliformes, which includes chickens, turkeys, and pheasants. The birds in this group have keels, and they will perform abrupt and fast flights, but only in extreme situations. Their feet are suitable for walking, running, and scratching the ground. This group includes the birds that human beings use the most. In general, females are in charge of incubating and raising the young.

1 Taking a run and jump

2 Clumsy and flapping fast

3 Emergency landing

Freshwater Birds

This group includes birds that vary greatly—from common
kingfishers to ducks to storks—and covers a wide spectrum.
Freshwater birds live in rivers, lakes, and ponds for at least part of
the year and are perfectly adapted to aquatic life. Some are excellent
swimmers, whereas others are great divers. An important group with
long legs wades in watercourses as they fish. Freshwater birds have a
varied diet and are mostly omnivorous.

Ducks and Distant Cousins

The order Anseriformes includes
birds that are very familiar to
humans: ducks, geese, and swans, for
example. They have short, webbed feet
and wide, flat bills lined with lamellae
(combs) that enable them to filter
their food, catch fish, and scrape the
beds of rivers and ponds. Most are
omnivorous and aquatic (either staying
on the surface or diving), although
some species spend more time on
land. They are widely distributed, and
the plumage of males becomes very
colorful during the courtship season.

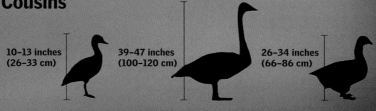

**10–13 inches
(26–33 cm)**

MUSCOVY DUCK
Cairina moschata

**39–47 inches
(100–120 cm)**

BLACK-NECKED SWAN
Cygnus melancoryphus

**26–34 inches
(66–86 cm)**

WHITE-FRONTED GOOSE
Anser albifrons

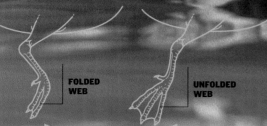

**FOLDED
WEB**

**UNFOLDED
WEB**

HOW THEY USE THEIR FEET TO SWIM

A duck moves its feet in two ways. To advance, it spreads out its toes and
uses its webbed feet to row. It closes the toes before bringing the foot
forward again. If the bird wants to turn, only one foot pushes to the side.

A DUCK'S DIET

1
It swims on the surface,
looking for food
underneath the water.

2
It sticks its head into the
water, abruptly pushes back
its feet, and turns its neck
downward.

3
It floats facedown and
pokes around on the
bottom with its bill.

ORIFICES
Open and oval

LAMELLAE
Comblike structures
around the inside
edges of the bill

DUCK BILLS

are flat, wide, and slightly depressed toward the middle.
In general, their shape does not vary much, but there are
species with tiny bills (the mandarin duck, for example).

**2–4 inches
(5–10 cm)**

**just over 1 inch
(2.7 cm)**

SHOVEL-SHAPED BILL:
Typical of many ducks. The
size varies.

MANDARIN DUCK BILL:
One of the smallest-billed
species.

**FULVOUS
WHISTLING
DUCK**
*Dendrocygna
bicolor*

Wading Birds

These birds belong to an artificial order since,
from a genetic perspective, the species are
not related. They are grouped together because
adaptation to the same habitat has caused them
to develop similar shapes: long bills and necks to
perform skillful movements and thin legs designed
to wade across the water as they fish. Herons form
a special group because they are cosmopolitan and
because they have powder down in their plumage. Ibis and
storks also have a wide distribution (area in which they
occur). Birds that have spoon- and hammer-shaped bills are
found primarily in Africa.

Divers and Other Fishers

Diving birds such as grebes feed on fish and aquatic insects. They are
excellent swimmers but clumsy on land as their legs are set so far back
on their body. Kingfishers find their prey by watching the water closely from
a perch above it, then diving in to spear the fish with their bills. Curlews,
sandpipers, and their relatives are shorebirds, wandering along the water's
edge in search of food. Their long legs keep their bodies out of the water. They
are not swimmers.

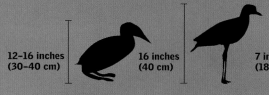

**12–16 inches
(30–40 cm)**

**16 inches
(40 cm)**

**7 inches
(18 cm)**

GREBE
Podiceps sp.

STONE CURLEW
Burhinus oedicnemus

**COMMON
KINGFISHER**
Alcedo atthis
(Also known as the
Eurasian Kingfisher)

DISCOVERY FACT™

Pelicans
have long bills
with lower mandibles
that open into huge
expandable pouches,
which they use to
scoop up fish as
they swim.

**THE BILL OF
AN IBIS**
is long and thin,
ideal to stick in
the mud to look
for food.

WHITE IBIS
Edocimus albus

IBIS (*Ibis* sp.):
Some filtrate, and others fish.

STORK (*Ciconia* sp.):
It fishes with its long bill.

SHOEBILL (*Balaeniceps rex*):
It eats among floating sedges.

HERON (*Egretta* sp.):
It fishes with its sharp bill.

COMMON SPOONBILL
(*Platalea leucorodia*): It eats
several types of aquatic animals.

HAMMERKOP (*Scopus
umbretta*): It fishes and hunts
small animals.

THE LEGS OF AN IBIS
keep the bird above the water
but close enough to fish. Ibis
also stir up the beds of lakes
and ponds.

Armed to Hunt

Birds of prey are hunters and are carnivorous by nature. They are perfectly equipped to eat living animals. Their eyesight is far sharper than that of human beings; their ears are designed to determine the precise status of their prey; they have strong, sharp talons; and they can kill a small mammal with the pressure of their talons alone. Their hook-shaped bills can kill prey by tearing its neck with a single peck. Eagles, falcons, vultures, and owls are examples of birds of prey. Birds of prey can be diurnal or nocturnal, and they are always on the lookout.

Diurnal and Nocturnal

Eagles, falcons, and vultures are diurnal birds of prey, whereas owls are nocturnal—that is, they are active during the night. These two groups are not closely related. These birds' main prey includes small mammals, reptiles, and insects. Once they locate the victim, they glide toward it. Nocturnal birds of prey are specially adapted: their eyesight is highly developed, their eyes are oriented forward, and their hearing is sharp. The feathers on their wings are arranged in such a way that they make no noise when the bird is flying. In order to protect themselves while sleeping during the day, they have dull plumage, which helps them blend in with their surroundings.

EURASIAN EAGLE OWL
Bubo bubo
Its ears are asymmetrical and can determine the location of prey with great precision.

BALD EAGLE
Haliaeetus leucocephalus
It has a visual field of 220 degrees and a bifocal vision of 50 degrees.

CERE
Fleshy formation, somewhat thick and soft

Bills

The bills of birds of prey are hook-shaped. Some species have a tooth that works like a knife, allowing them to kill their prey, tear its skin and muscle tissues, and get to the food easily. The structure and shape of the bills of birds of prey varies, depending on the species. Scavengers (for example, vultures and condors) have weaker bills because the tissues of animals in decomposition are softer. Other species, such as falcons, catch prey with their talons and use their bills to finish it off with a violent stab to the neck, breaking its spine.

TIP
Where the tooth is located

NOSTRIL
Olfactory canals

Zone-tailed Hawk
Buteo albonotatus

BALD EAGLE
Its hooked bill is a shape common to many birds of prey.

SPARROW HAWK
Its thin bill enables it to extract snails from their shells.

FALCON
It can break the spine of its prey with its upper bill.

GOSHAWK
Its strong bill means that it can catch prey as large as hares.

OWL PELLETS

Owls produce pellets. They swallow their prey whole and regurgitate the indigestible substances. The study of pellets makes it possible to determine the fauna of small areas with great precision.

HOW VULTURES HUNT

1 Vultures feed mainly on carrion, although they are able to attack a living animal if it is vulnerable and the situation presents itself.

2 Thanks to their ability to glide on thermals, vultures can find carcasses on which to feed without wasting energy.

3 Once they find food, they must analyze the territory to know if they will be able to take flight again soon.

DISCOVERY FACT™

The eyesight of raptors is up to eight times sharper than ours, and a golden eagle can spot its prey from 1 mile (1.6 km) away.

DIMENSIONS

The wings of birds of prey are adapted to suit their flying requirements. They can measure up to 10 feet (3 m).

CONDORS
3–9½ feet (0.95–2.9 m)

EAGLES
4½–8 feet (1.35–2.45 m)

BUZZARDS
4–5 feet (1.2–1.5 m)

KITES
2½–6½ feet (0.8–1.95 m)

RED-BACKED HAWK
3½–4½ feet (1.05–1.35 m)

FALCONS
2¼–4 feet (0.67–1.25 m)

Feet

Most birds of prey catch and kill their prey with their talons and tear away the meat with their bills. For this reason, birds' feet constitute one of the morphological characteristics of a species. The toes end in strong, sharp claws that the bird uses as pincers to catch its prey in flight. The osprey also has barbs on its feet, which help it to grip slippery fish.

GRIFFON VULTURE
Its long toes do not have a good grasp.

FISH HAWK
Its toes have rough scales like barbs, which help it to catch and hold on to fish.

GOSHAWK
It has calluses at the tips of its toes.

SPARROW HAWK
Its feet have tarsi and short, strong toes.

The Perchers Club

Passerines—perching birds—form the largest, most diverse order of birds. What distinguishes them? Their feet are suited for perching and, therefore, for living among trees, although they can also stroll on the ground and through brush. They inhabit terrestrial environments all over the world, from deserts to woodlands. Their complex sounds and songs originate from a very well-developed vocal organ called a "syrinx." Their chicks are nidicolous—that is, naked and blind at birth. In youth, they are agile and vivacious, with very attractive, abundant, and colorful plumage.

DISCOVERY FACT™

The songbird's syrinx is at the base of the trachea, where it forks into the lungs, allowing some birds to produce more than one sound at a time.

The Smallest

Passerines are small in comparison with other birds. They range in size from tiny bee hummingbirds (*Mellisuga helenae*) to the heavily built common raven (*Corvus corax*).

HUMMINGBIRDS
2 INCHES (5 CM)
They get so much energy from nectar that they can double their body weight by eating. However, they use this energy up during their frantic flights.

SWALLOWS
7 INCHES (19 CM)
Swallows have great agility and skill. These popular migratory birds have bodies suited for long journeys.

RAVENS
26 INCHES (65 CM)
They eat everything: fruits, insects, reptiles, small mammals, and birds. They are skillful robbers of all kinds of food.

PASSERIFORMES

Passerines have been classified into 79 families, with more than 5,400 different species.

50%
THE PERCENTAGE OF BIRDS INCLUDED IN THE ORDER PASSERIFORMES.

Family Album

Four basic groups have been established to facilitate the study of families: broadbills, passerines with wide bills; ovenbirds, with dull, brown plumage, noted for the great care they take in building their nests; lyrebirds, whose tails have two showy external feathers that are longer than the others; and songbirds, with their elaborate and pleasant singing. Songbirds form the most numerous and varied group, which includes swallows, goldfinches, canaries, vireos, and ravens.

LYREBIRDS
There are only two species of these Passeriformes, and they are found only in Australia. They are very melodic and are excellent imitators of other birds. They can even imitate the sound of inanimate objects, such as motors or cellphones.

HARD, SHORT BILL
The bill of a swallow is very short and tough. The swallow can use it to catch insects in flight.

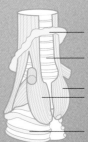

SINGER
This blue-and-white swallow (*Notiochelidon cyanoleuca*) intones its pleasant and trilling chant in flight and while perching. Larks, goldfinches, canaries, and other passerines delight us with their trills and songs.

SYRINX
This organ is the equivalent of the human larynx, but has no vocal cords. The syrinx muscles move the bronchial walls, which, as air passes through, produce the melodic sounds that characterize songbirds.

SYRINGEAL CARTILAGE

TRACHEAL RING

BRONCHIAL MUSCLES

BRONCHIAL RING

LIVING AT THE EXTREMES
Swallows range from one hemisphere to the other. They raise their chicks in the north and fly to the south to spend winter there, traveling all the way to Tierra del Fuego. Their sense of direction is remarkable. They can find and reuse their nests after returning from a migration.

A In the summer, during the reproductive season, they live in the Northern Hemisphere on the North American continent. In general, neotropical migratory birds are those that reproduce above the Tropic of Cancer.

B When winter arrives in the Northern Hemisphere, they perform a mass migration to the south, occupying the Caribbean and South America. The barn swallow travels 14,000 miles (22,000 km) during its migratory trip from the United States to southern Argentina.

PERCHING FOOT
Three toes project forward, and the well-developed hallux projects backward. This type of foot allows the bird to hold on tightly to branches.

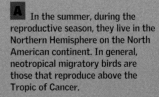

BARN SWALLOW
(*Hirundo rustica*)
Barn swallows spend most of their time traveling to temperate zones.

BROADBILLS
They are native to Africa and Asia and inhabit tropical zones with dense vegetation. They eat insects and fruits. They produce nonvocal sounds with the flapping of their wings. They do this during courtship, and the sound can be heard 200 feet (60 m) away.

OVENBIRDS AND THEIR RELATIVES
Ovenbird nests are completely covered structures, built from clay. Other members of this family build nests with leaves and straw, weaving interesting baskets. Still others dig tunnels in the ground.

Skin with Scales

Reptiles are vertebrates, meaning that they are animals with a spinal column. Their skin is hard, dry, and flaky. Like birds, most reptiles are born from eggs deposited on land. The offspring hatch fully formed without passing through a larval stage. The first reptiles appeared during the height of the Carboniferous period in the Paleozoic era. During the Mesozoic era, they evolved and flourished, which is why this period is also known as the age of reptiles. Only 5 of the 23 orders that existed then have living representatives today.

SOLOMON ISLAND SKINK
Corucia zebrata

EMBRIONIC MEMBRANES
All reptiles develop two: a protective amnion (egg sac) and a respiratory allantois (vascular fetal membrane).

EYES
are almost always small. In diurnal animals, the pupil is rounded.

NICTITATING MEMBRANE
It extends from the internal angle of the eye to cover the eyeball.

4,765
SPECIES OF LIZARDS EXIST.

BLACK CAIMAN
Melanosuchus niger

Habitat

Reptiles have a great capacity to adapt, because they can occupy an incredible variety of environments. They live on every continent except Antarctica, and most countries have at least one species of terrestrial reptile. They can be found in the driest and hottest deserts, as well as the steamiest, most humid rain forests. They are especially common in the tropical and subtropical regions of Africa, Asia, Australia, and the Americas, where high temperatures and a great diversity of prey allow them to thrive.

Crocodiles

are distinguished by their usually large size. From neck to tail, their backs are covered in rows of bony plates, which can resemble spikes or teeth. Crocodiles appeared toward the end of the Triassic period, and they are the closest living relatives to both dinosaurs and birds. Their hearts are divided into four chambers, their brains show a high degree of development, and the musculature of their abdomens is so developed that it resembles the gizzards of birds. The larger species are very dangerous.

OVIPAROUS
Most reptiles are oviparous (they lay eggs); however, many species of snakes and lizards are ovoviviparous (they produce eggs that develop within the mother's body and give birth to live offspring).

THORAX AND ABDOMEN
are not separated by a diaphragm. Alligators breathe with the help of muscles on the walls of their body.

AMERICAN ALLIGATOR
Alligator mississippiensis

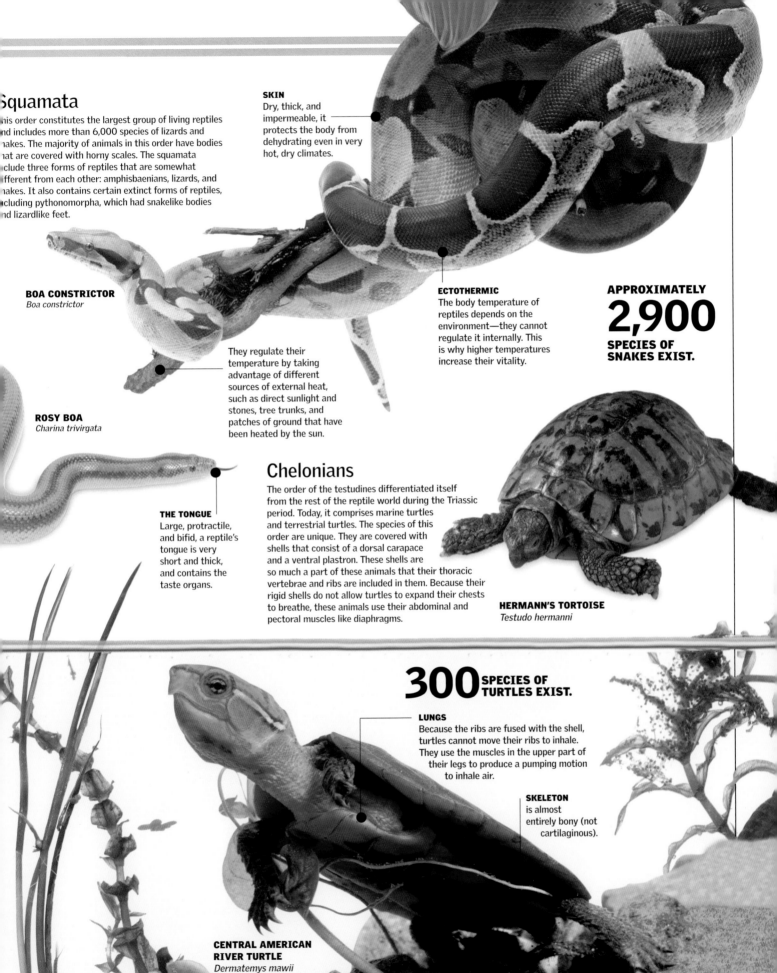

Squamata

This order constitutes the largest group of living reptiles and includes more than 6,000 species of lizards and snakes. The majority of animals in this order have bodies that are covered with horny scales. The squamata include three forms of reptiles that are somewhat different from each other: amphisbaenians, lizards, and snakes. It also contains certain extinct forms of reptiles, including pythonomorpha, which had snakelike bodies and lizardlike feet.

SKIN
Dry, thick, and impermeable, it protects the body from dehydrating even in very hot, dry climates.

BOA CONSTRICTOR
Boa constrictor

ECTOTHERMIC
The body temperature of reptiles depends on the environment—they cannot regulate it internally. This is why higher temperatures increase their vitality.

They regulate their temperature by taking advantage of different sources of external heat, such as direct sunlight and stones, tree trunks, and patches of ground that have been heated by the sun.

ROSY BOA
Charina trivirgata

APPROXIMATELY
2,900
SPECIES OF SNAKES EXIST.

THE TONGUE
Large, protractile, and bifid, a reptile's tongue is very short and thick, and contains the taste organs.

Chelonians

The order of the testudines differentiated itself from the rest of the reptile world during the Triassic period. Today, it comprises marine turtles and terrestrial turtles. The species of this order are unique. They are covered with shells that consist of a dorsal carapace and a ventral plastron. These shells are so much a part of these animals that their thoracic vertebrae and ribs are included in them. Because their rigid shells do not allow turtles to expand their chests to breathe, these animals use their abdominal and pectoral muscles like diaphragms.

HERMANN'S TORTOISE
Testudo hermanni

300 SPECIES OF TURTLES EXIST.

LUNGS
Because the ribs are fused with the shell, turtles cannot move their ribs to inhale. They use the muscles in the upper part of their legs to produce a pumping motion to inhale air.

SKELETON
is almost entirely bony (not cartilaginous).

CENTRAL AMERICAN RIVER TURTLE
Dermatemys mawii

Lizards

Lizards are the largest group of reptiles. They live in most environments except for extremely cold regions, because they cannot regulate their own body temperatures. There are land-dwelling, underground, tree-dwelling, and even semiaquatic lizards. They can walk, climb, dig, run, and even glide. Most lizards have differentiated heads, movable eyelids, a rigid lower jaw, four five-toed feet, a long body covered with scales, and a long tail. Some can even shed their tails when threatened.

DAY GECKO
Phelsuma sp.

DISCOVERY FACT™

If a lizard sheds its tail to escape a predator, the tail goes on wiggling to fool the attacker into thinking it is still holding the whole lizard.

STICKY TOES

Chameleons

live in Africa, especially in southeastern regions and on Madagascar. They live in forests, where they use their prehensile tails and toes to climb trees. Their well-known ability to change color is important when they face danger or during courtship.

Camouflage

is an adaptive advantage. By blending in with the vegetation surrounding them, lizards can escape the notice of both their predators and their prey.

LIFESAVING MEASURE
Between each vertebra, there are rupture planes enabling the tail to separate from the body.

AUTOTOMIC TAIL
Certain lizards can shed their tails many times during their lives. In dangerous situations, they may even shed it voluntarily in order to flee a confused predator. Later, the tail grows back.

TELESCOPIC EYES

Geckos and Skinks

are lizardlike animals of the family Gekkonidae that live in warm regions. Their limbs are very small, or even nonexistent in some species. Their bodies are covered with smooth, shiny scales.

MELLER'S CHAMELEON
Chamaeleo melleri

SKIN
has cells with many pigments.

TAIL
curls up when necessary.

PREHENSILE TOES
can surround a branch and hold on tight.

CLAW

4,765
LIZARD SPECIES EXIST IN THE WORLD.

Heloderma

comprise only two species, which live in the United States and Mexico. They feed on invertebrates and small vertebrates. Their bodies are massive, and their skin is covered with small knobs. They are the only poisonous lizards, and their bite can be dangerous to humans.

COLORS
warn of poison.

GILA MONSTER
Heloderma suspectum

FAT TAIL
stores fat reserves for later consumption.

NOSTRIL

EYE WITH EYELID

EAR

MOUTH

CREST
runs from head to tail.

SKIN
has scales covered with a tough, hornlike layer.

SUBTYMPANIC SHIELD
is a large scale resembling an eye, possibly to deter predators.

DEWLAP
is fleshy and large in males.

CREST

COMMON IGUANA
Iguana sp.

Body Heat

Lizards survive in environments where they can maintain their body temperature, such as forests or deserts.

SUNBATHING 6:00 AM
The lizard places its body in the Sun's rays to take advantage of their heat.

IN ACTION 10:00 AM
It begins its daily activities and movements.

HIDDEN 12:00 PM
When the Sun is at its highest, the lizard hides from excessive heat.

CATCHING A FEW MORE RAYS 6:00 PM
It returns to the sunlight but elevates its body to take advantage of the heat radiating from the rocks.

Iguanas

Iguanas belong to the largest New World group of reptiles and have the most complex design. They inhabit tropical regions of the Americas, including the forests of Mexico. They can change color during the mating season. The species of this group are vegetarians.

FEET WITH CLAWS
enable it to walk, climb, and dig burrows.

Venerated and Feared

Crocodiles—along with their relatives, the alligators, caimans, and gharials—are very ancient animals. They belong to the same group that included the dinosaurs and have changed very little in the last 65 million years. They can go for long periods without moving; during these times, they sun themselves or rest in the water. However, they can also swim, jump, and even run at high speed to attack with force and precision. In spite of their ferocity, female crocodilians provide more care for their young than any other living group of reptiles.

LOWER JAW
The lower teeth are invisible when the mouth is closed.

SCALES
are flat on the tail.

GHARIAL
Gavialis gangeticus

HABITAT	Freshwater
NUMBER OF TYPES	One
DEGREE OF DANGER	Harmless

— 13-23 feet (4-7 m) —

The Gharial

is the strangest of all crocodilians. Its long, narrow snout, with small, sharp teeth, sweeps through the water. Its interlocked, outward-curving teeth are perfect for catching slippery fish. Adult males drive away their rivals with loud buzzing sounds that they make by exhaling air through a bump on their nose.

GHARIAL
has a long, narrow snout, with long front teeth.

CROCODILE
has a V-shaped snout, narrower than the alligator's.

ALLIGATOR
has a wide, short, U-shaped nose.

TEETH
are longest in front.

SNOUT
Long, narrow nose

1 It moves forward with its four limbs.

The front legs begin the movement.

2 Its legs are suspended.

Then the hind legs come into action.

3 The cycle starts over.

The tail is raised to avoid acting as a brake.

9 miles per hour (15 km/h)
IS THE SPEED THEY CAN REACH AT A FULL RUN.

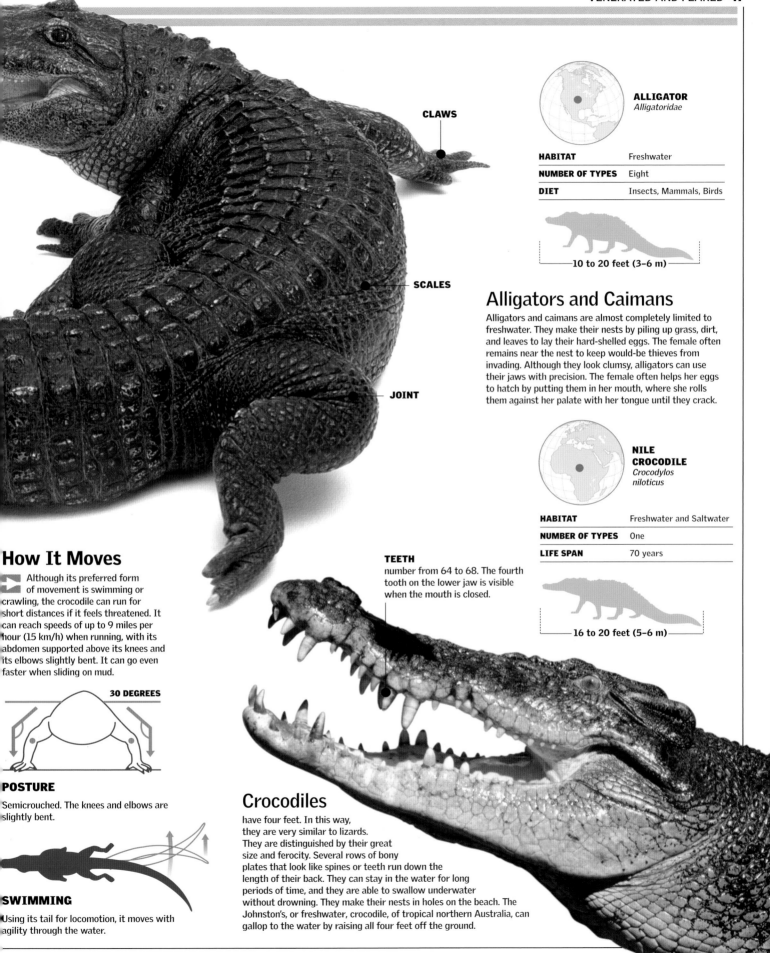

CLAWS

SCALES

JOINT

ALLIGATOR
Alligatoridae

HABITAT	Freshwater
NUMBER OF TYPES	Eight
DIET	Insects, Mammals, Birds

10 to 20 feet (3–6 m)

Alligators and Caimans

Alligators and caimans are almost completely limited to freshwater. They make their nests by piling up grass, dirt, and leaves to lay their hard-shelled eggs. The female often remains near the nest to keep would-be thieves from invading. Although they look clumsy, alligators can use their jaws with precision. The female often helps her eggs to hatch by putting them in her mouth, where she rolls them against her palate with her tongue until they crack.

NILE CROCODILE
Crocodylos niloticus

HABITAT	Freshwater and Saltwater
NUMBER OF TYPES	One
LIFE SPAN	70 years

16 to 20 feet (5–6 m)

TEETH
number from 64 to 68. The fourth tooth on the lower jaw is visible when the mouth is closed.

How It Moves

Although its preferred form of movement is swimming or crawling, the crocodile can run for short distances if it feels threatened. It can reach speeds of up to 9 miles per hour (15 km/h) when running, with its abdomen supported above its knees and its elbows slightly bent. It can go even faster when sliding on mud.

30 DEGREES

POSTURE

Semicrouched. The knees and elbows are slightly bent.

SWIMMING

Using its tail for locomotion, it moves with agility through the water.

Crocodiles

have four feet. In this way, they are very similar to lizards. They are distinguished by their great size and ferocity. Several rows of bony plates that look like spines or teeth run down the length of their back. They can stay in the water for long periods of time, and they are able to swallow underwater without drowning. They make their nests in holes on the beach. The Johnston's, or freshwater, crocodile, of tropical northern Australia, can gallop to the water by raising all four feet off the ground.

Dangerous Coils

S nakes are scaly reptiles with long bodies and no legs. Some are poisonous, but others are not. Like all reptiles, they have a skeletal structure and a spinal column composed of a system of vertebrae. The anatomical differences between species reveal information about their habitats and diets—climbing snakes are long and thin, burrowing snakes are shorter and thicker, and sea snakes have flat tails that they use as fins.

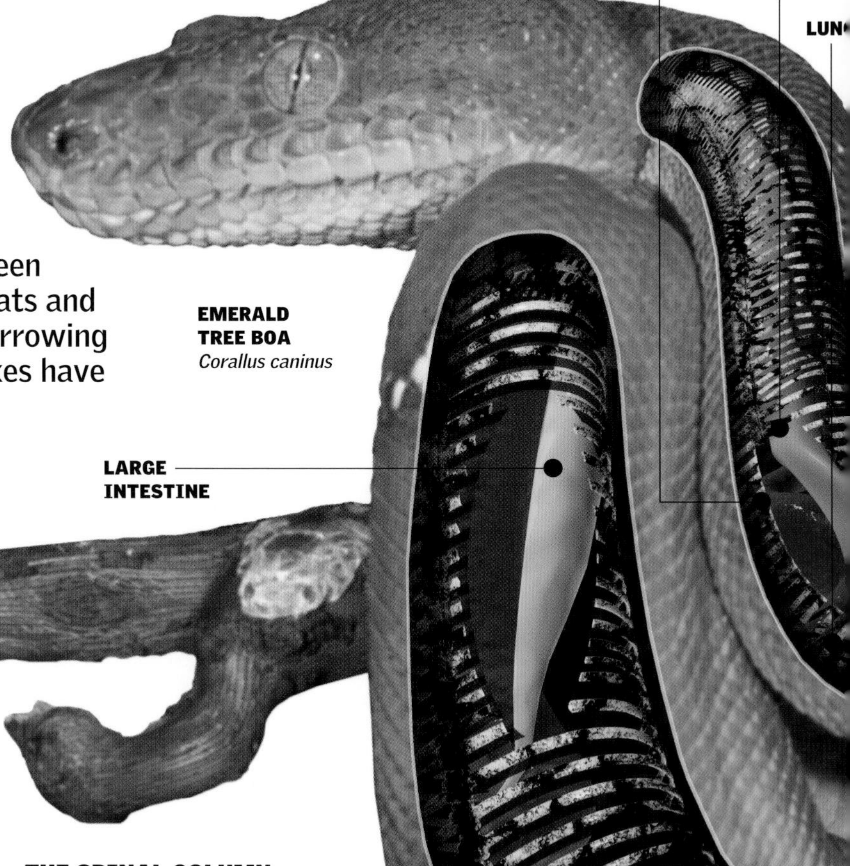

COLD-BLOODED
Their temperature varies according to the environment. They do not generate their own body heat.

HEART
The ventricle has an incomplete partition.

ESOPHAGUS

LUN

EMERALD TREE BOA
Corallus caninus

LARGE INTESTINE

TREE BRANCH
Boas can change color to imitate the branch they are curled around.

Primitive Snakes

Boas and pythons were the first snake species to appear on Earth. Many have claws or spurs as vestiges of the ancient limbs of their ancestors. They are not poisonous, but they are the largest and strongest snakes. They live in trees, and some, such as the anaconda—a South American boa—live in rivers.

33 feet
(10 m)
THE LENGTH OF A PYTHON.

SPOTTED PYTHON
Antaresia maculosa inhabits the forests of Australia.

THE SPINAL COLUMN
is composed of an assembly of jointed vertebrae with prolongations that protect the nerves and arteries. The system makes them enormously flexible.

VERTEBRAE

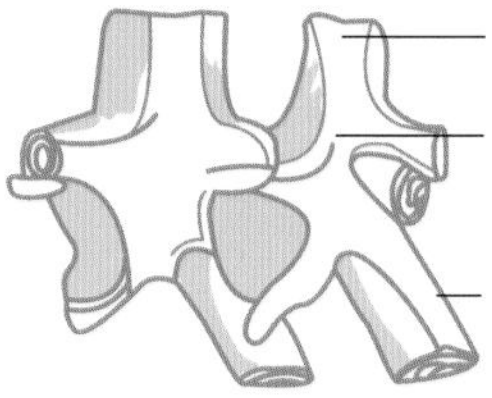

NEURAL ARCH

BODY OF THE VERTEBRA

HEMAL KEEL

FLOATING RIBS
allow the body to increase in size.

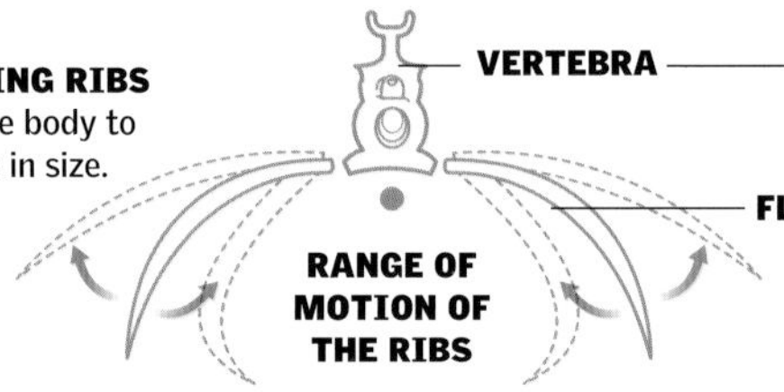

VERTEBRA

FLOATING RIB

RANGE OF MOTION OF THE RIBS

400 vertebrae THE NUMBER A SNAKE CAN HAVE

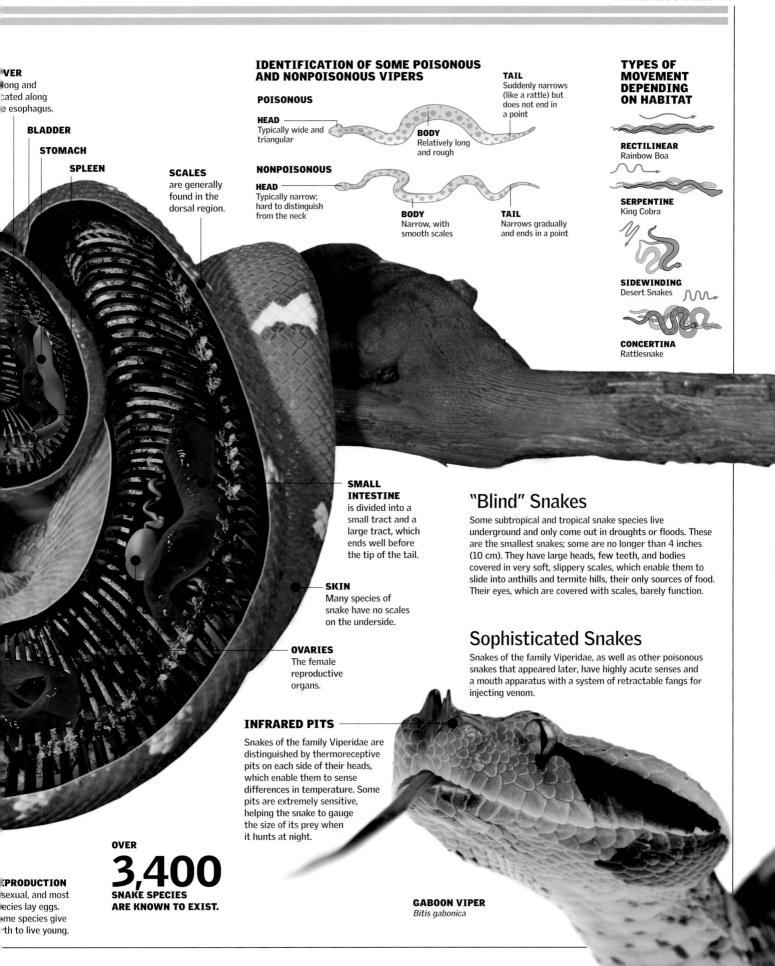

VER
long and
cated along
e esophagus.

BLADDER

STOMACH

SPLEEN

SCALES
are generally
found in the
dorsal region.

IDENTIFICATION OF SOME POISONOUS AND NONPOISONOUS VIPERS

POISONOUS

HEAD
Typically wide and
triangular

BODY
Relatively long
and rough

TAIL
Suddenly narrows
(like a rattle) but
does not end in
a point

NONPOISONOUS

HEAD
Typically narrow;
hard to distinguish
from the neck

BODY
Narrow, with
smooth scales

TAIL
Narrows gradually
and ends in a point

TYPES OF MOVEMENT DEPENDING ON HABITAT

RECTILINEAR
Rainbow Boa

SERPENTINE
King Cobra

SIDEWINDING
Desert Snakes

CONCERTINA
Rattlesnake

SMALL INTESTINE
is divided into a
small tract and a
large tract, which
ends well before
the tip of the tail.

SKIN
Many species of
snake have no scales
on the underside.

OVARIES
The female
reproductive
organs.

INFRARED PITS

Snakes of the family Viperidae are
distinguished by thermoreceptive
pits on each side of their heads,
which enable them to sense
differences in temperature. Some
pits are extremely sensitive,
helping the snake to gauge
the size of its prey when
it hunts at night.

"Blind" Snakes

Some subtropical and tropical snake species live
underground and only come out in droughts or floods. These
are the smallest snakes; some are no longer than 4 inches
(10 cm). They have large heads, few teeth, and bodies
covered in very soft, slippery scales, which enable them to
slide into anthills and termite hills, their only sources of food.
Their eyes, which are covered with scales, barely function.

Sophisticated Snakes

Snakes of the family Viperidae, as well as other poisonous
snakes that appeared later, have highly acute senses and
a mouth apparatus with a system of retractable fangs for
injecting venom.

OVER
3,400
**SNAKE SPECIES
ARE KNOWN TO EXIST.**

EPRODUCTION
sexual, and most
ecies lay eggs.
me species give
rth to live young.

GABOON VIPER
Bitis gabonica

Fishy Features

Similar characteristics define nearly all fish, with a few rare exceptions. These aquatic animals are designed to live underwater, and they have a jawbone and lidless eyes and are cold-blooded. They breathe through gills and are vertebrates—that is, they have a spinal column. They live in the oceans, from the poles to the Equator, as well as in bodies of freshwater and in streams. Some fish migrate, but very few can pass from salt water to freshwater or vice versa. Their fins enable them to swim and move in different directions. Marine animals such as dolphins, seals, and whales are at times mistaken for fish, but they are actually mammals.

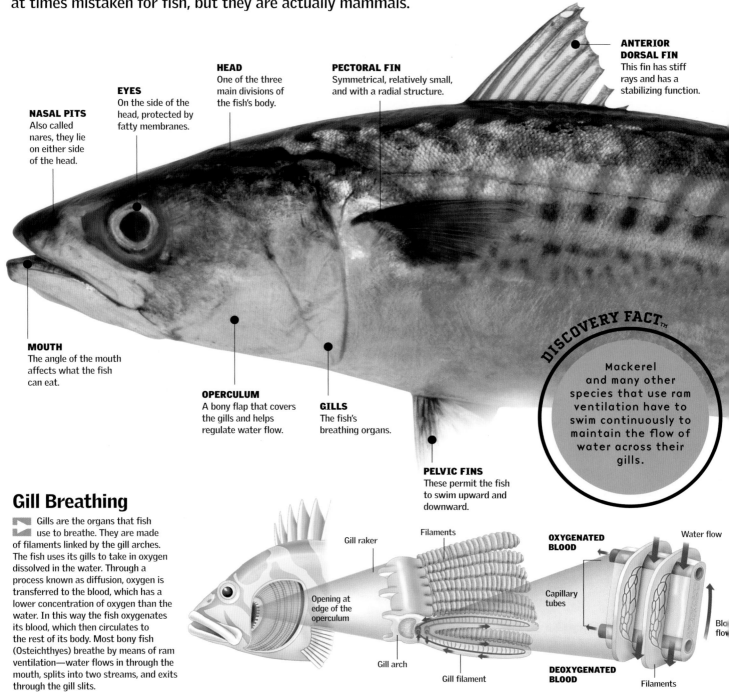

ANTERIOR DORSAL FIN
This fin has stiff rays and has a stabilizing function.

HEAD
One of the three main divisions of the fish's body.

PECTORAL FIN
Symmetrical, relatively small, and with a radial structure.

EYES
On the side of the head, protected by fatty membranes.

NASAL PITS
Also called nares, they lie on either side of the head.

MOUTH
The angle of the mouth affects what the fish can eat.

OPERCULUM
A bony flap that covers the gills and helps regulate water flow.

GILLS
The fish's breathing organs.

PELVIC FINS
These permit the fish to swim upward and downward.

DISCOVERY FACT™

Mackerel and many other species that use ram ventilation have to swim continuously to maintain the flow of water across their gills.

Gill Breathing

Gills are the organs that fish use to breathe. They are made of filaments linked by the gill arches. The fish uses its gills to take in oxygen dissolved in the water. Through a process known as diffusion, oxygen is transferred to the blood, which has a lower concentration of oxygen than the water. In this way the fish oxygenates its blood, which then circulates to the rest of its body. Most bony fish (Osteichthyes) breathe by means of ram ventilation—water flows in through the mouth, splits into two streams, and exits through the gill slits.

Gill raker

Filaments

OXYGENATED BLOOD

Water flow

Opening at edge of the operculum

Capillary tubes

Gill arch

Gill filament

DEOXYGENATED BLOOD

Filaments

Blood flow

Near fossils

Choanichthyes (Sarcopterygii) are archaic bony fish with fleshy fins. Some of them were the first animals to have lungs. Only a few species survive.

COELACANTH

Latimeria chalumnae
This species was thought to have gone extinct millions of years ago, until one was discovered alive off the coast of South Africa in 1938; more of these fish were found later.

Jawless Fish

Of the ancient Agnathans, considered the first living vertebrates, only lampreys and hagfish are left.

SEA LAMPREY

Lampetra sp.
Its round, toothed mouth allows it to suck the blood of fish of various species. There are also freshwater lampreys.

Just Cartilage

Cartilaginous fish, such as rays and sharks, have extremely flexible skeletons with little or no bone.

RAY

Raja miraletus
Its large fins send currents of water carrying plankton and small fish to its mouth. The ray is very fast.

SCALES

The scales are imbricate—that is, they overlap one another.

POSTERIOR DORSAL FIN

This soft-structured fin is located between the dorsal fin and the tail.

LATERAL LINE

Fish have sensory organs all along this line.

With Spines

Osteichthyes is the most numerous class of fish. The skeleton has some level of calcification.

ATLANTIC MACKEREL

Scomber scombrus
This fish has no teeth. It lives in temperate waters, and its meat is considered delicious. It can live for more than ten years.

ANAL FIN

Soft, with a row of finlets

TAIL MUSCLE

This is the strongest muscle in the fish.

CAUDAL FIN

It moves from side to side, propelling the fish forward.

IN ACTION

Water enters the mouth and flows over the gills. After the gills extract oxygen, the water is expelled through the gill slits.

OPERCULUM

Opens and closes the openings where water exits

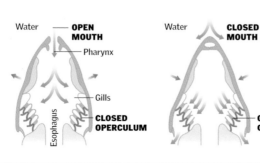

Water | **OPEN MOUTH**
Pharynx
Gills
Esophagus
CLOSED OPERCULUM

Water | **CLOSED MOUTH**
OPEN OPERCULUM

OVER
28,000

IS THE NUMBER OF KNOWN FISH SPECIES, MAKING UP NEARLY ONE HALF OF ALL CHORDATE SPECIES.

The Art of Swimming

To swim, fish move in three dimensions: forward and back, left and right, and up and down. The main control surfaces that fish use for maneuvering are the fins, including the tail, or caudal, fin. To change direction, the fish tilts the control surfaces at an angle to the water current. The fish must also keep its balance in the water; it accomplishes this by moving its paired and unpaired fins.

UPSIDE-DOWN CATFISH
Synodontis nigriventris
This fish swims upside down, seeking food sources that are less accessible to other species.

MUSCLES

The tail has powerful muscles that enable it to move like an oar.

GREAT WHITE SHARK
Carcharodon carcharias

RED MUSCLES
are for slow or regular movements.

LARGER WHITE MUSCLES
are for moving with speed, but they tire easily.

 ## Starting Out

The movement of a fish through the water is like that of a slithering snake. Its body goes through a series of wavelike movements similar to an S curve. This process begins when the fish moves its head slightly from side to side.

The crest of the body's wave moves from back to front.

In its side-to-side movement, the tail displaces the water.

At first, the tail is even with the head.

Streamlined Shape

Like the keel of a ship, the rounded contours of a fish are instrumental. In addition, most of a fish's volume is in the front part of its body. As the fish swims forward, its shape causes the density of the water ahead to be reduced relative to the density of the water behind. This reduces the water's resistance.

The head moves from side to side.

THE FISH'S KEEL

A ship has a heavy keel in the lower part to keep it from capsizing. Fish, on the other hand, have the keel on top. If the paired fins stop functioning to keep the fish balanced, the fish turns over because its heaviest part tends to sink, which happens when fish die.

KEEL

LIVE FISH **DEAD FISH**

THE FASTEST

The powerful caudal fin displaces large amounts of water.

SAILFISH
Istiophorus platypterus

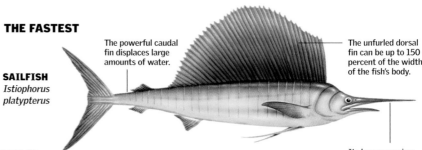

The unfurled dorsal fin can be up to 150 percent of the width of the fish's body.

Its long upper jaw enables it to slice through the water, aiding this fish's hydrodynamics.

70 miles per hour
(109 km/h) THE MAXIMUM SWIMMING SPEED IT ATTAINS.

Forward Motion

results from the synchronized S-curve movement of the muscles surrounding the spinal column. These muscles usually make alternating lateral motions. Fish with large pectoral fins use them like oars for propulsion.

The oarlike movement of the tail is the main force used for forward motion.

THE DORSAL FIN keeps the fish upright.

THE PECTORAL FINS maintain balance and can act as brakes.

THE VENTRAL FINS stabilize the fish for proper balance.

Balance

When the fish is moving slowly or is still in the water, the fins can be seen making small movements to keep the body in balance.

Upward and Downward

The angle of the fins relative to the body allows the fish to move up or down. The paired fins, located in front of the center of gravity, are used for this upward or downward movement.

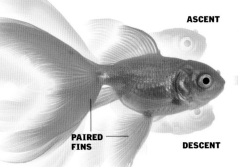

ASCENT

PAIRED FINS

DESCENT

2 Forceful Stroke

Muscles on both sides of the spinal column, especially the tail muscles, contract in an alternating pattern. These contractions power the wavelike movement that propels the fish forward. The crest of the wave reaches the pelvic and dorsal fins.

The crest of the wave passes to the first dorsal fins.

When the crest reaches the area between the two dorsal fins, the tail fin begins its push to the right.

3 Complete Cycle

When the tail moves back toward the other side and reaches the far right, the head will once again turn to the right to begin a new cycle.

The resulting impulse moves the fish forward.

1 second

THE TIME IT TAKES FOR THIS SHARK TO COMPLETE ONE SWIMMING CYCLE.

CAT SHARK
Scyliorhinus sp.

1 cubic mile (4 cu km)

THE AREA THAT CAN BE TAKEN UP BY A SCHOOL OF HERRING.

SCHOOL
A group of fish, usually of the same species, that swim together in a coordinated manner and with specific individual roles.

Swimming in Groups

Only bony fish can swim in highly coordinated groups. Schools or shoals of fish include thousands of individuals that move harmoniously as if they were a single fish. To coordinate their motion, they use their sight, hearing, and lateral line senses. Swimming in groups has its advantages: it is harder to be caught by a predator, and it is easier to find companions or food.

DISCOVERY FACT™

Imaging technology called Ocean Acoustic Waveguide Remote Sensing has detected megashoals of hundred of millions of herring in the Atlantic.

The fish on the outside, guided by those in the middle, are in charge of keeping the group safe.

The fish in the middle control the group.

Deadly Weapon

One of the greatest predators in the ocean is the great white shark, easily identified by its distinctive white coloring, black eyes, and fierce teeth and jaws. Many biologists believe that attacks on humans result from the shark's exploratory behavior, because these fish often lift their heads above the water and explore things by biting them. This activity is often dangerous because of the sharpness of the sharks' teeth and the strength of their jaws. Great white sharks are implicated in most fatal shark attacks on humans, especially on surfers and divers.

Senses

Sharks have senses that most animals lack. The ampullae of Lorenzini are small clefts in the shark's head that detect electricity. This sense helps them find prey hidden in the sand. The lateral line is used to detect movement or sound underwater. Smell is their most advanced sense, and it occupies two thirds of their brain. They also have a highly developed sense of hearing, which allows them to detect very low-frequency sounds.

HEARING
Detects sounds of very low frequency.

AMPULLAE OF LORENZINI
Detect nerve impulses.

NOSE
The most highly developed sense is smell; it takes up two thirds of the brain.

LATERAL LINE
Detects movements or sounds underwater.

ELECTRIC RADAR

CAUDAL FIN
The great white shark has a large heterocercal caudal fin.

GREAT WHITE SHARK
Carcharodon carcharias

HABITAT	Oceans
WEIGHT	4,400 pounds (2,000 kg)
LENGTH	23 feet (7 m)
LIFE SPAN	30–40 years

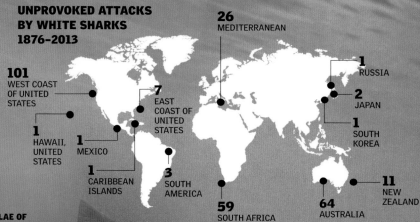

UNPROVOKED ATTACKS BY WHITE SHARKS 1876–2013

26 MEDITERRANEAN

101 WEST COAST OF UNITED STATES

7 EAST COAST OF UNITED STATES

1 RUSSIA

2 JAPAN

1 SOUTH KOREA

1 HAWAII, UNITED STATES

1 MEXICO

1 CARIBBEAN ISLANDS

3 SOUTH AMERICA

59 SOUTH AFRICA

64 AUSTRALIA

11 NEW ZEALAND

280
INCLUDING 77 FATAL ATTACKS.

NASAL PITS

EYES
Sharks have poor vision and use their sense of smell to hunt.

JAW
During an attack, it stretches forward.

DORSAL FIN

ANAL FIN

PECTORAL FIN
Highly developed and very important for swimming.

PELVIC FIN

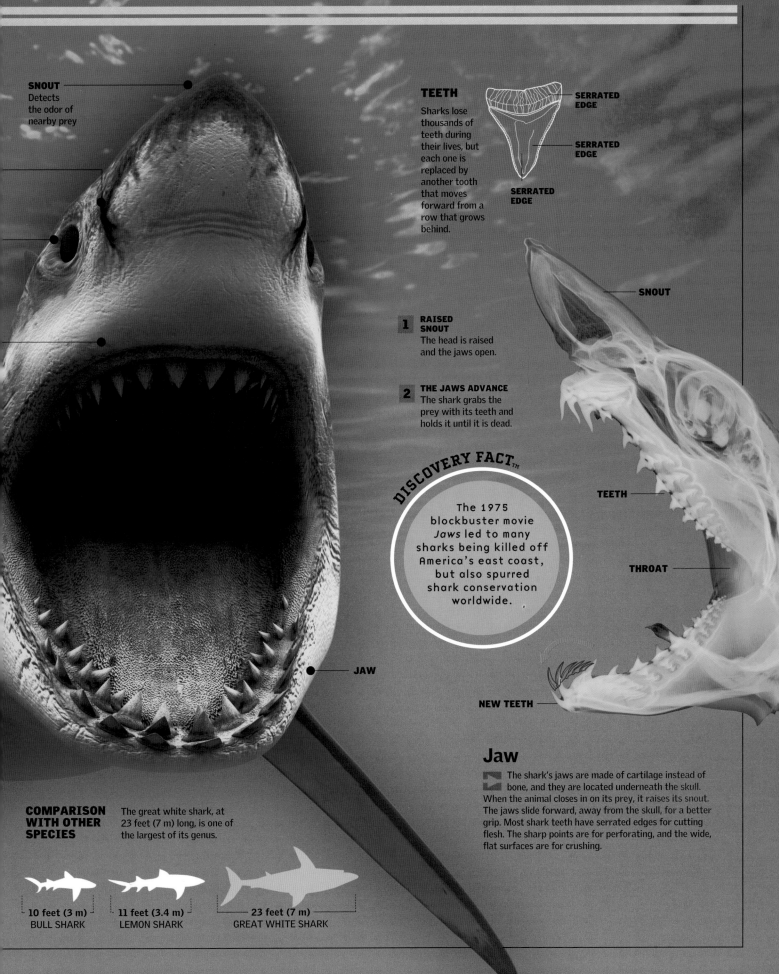

SNOUT
Detects the odor of nearby prey

TEETH
Sharks lose thousands of teeth during their lives, but each one is replaced by another tooth that moves forward from a row that grows behind.

SERRATED EDGE

SERRATED EDGE

SERRATED EDGE

SNOUT

1 RAISED SNOUT
The head is raised and the jaws open.

2 THE JAWS ADVANCE
The shark grabs the prey with its teeth and holds it until it is dead.

TEETH

DISCOVERY FACT™

The 1975 blockbuster movie *Jaws* led to many sharks being killed off America's east coast, but also spurred shark conservation worldwide.

THROAT

JAW

NEW TEETH

Jaw

The shark's jaws are made of cartilage instead of bone, and they are located underneath the skull. When the animal closes in on its prey, it raises its snout. The jaws slide forward, away from the skull, for a better grip. Most shark teeth have serrated edges for cutting flesh. The sharp points are for perforating, and the wide, flat surfaces are for crushing.

COMPARISON WITH OTHER SPECIES
The great white shark, at 23 feet (7 m) long, is one of the largest of its genus.

10 feet (3 m)
BULL SHARK

11 feet (3.4 m)
LEMON SHARK

23 feet (7 m)
GREAT WHITE SHARK

The Journey Home

After living in the ocean for five or six years, the Pacific red salmon (*Oncorhynchus nerka*) returns to the river where it was born to reproduce. The journey lasts around three months, and demands a great deal of energy. The salmon must swim against the current, climb waterfalls, and evade predators, including bears and eagles. Once the salmon reach the river, the female lays her eggs, and the male fertilizes them. Typically, the same locations in specific rivers are sought year after year. This species of salmon dies after completing the reproductive cycle, unlike the Atlantic salmon, which repeats the cycle three or four times. Once the eggs hatch, the cycle begins anew.

■ ASIA ■ ALASKA ■ UNITED STATES

The Route

There are six species of salmon in the Pacific Ocean and one in the Atlantic. The red salmon (*Oncorhynchus nerka*) migrates from the Pacific Ocean to the rivers of the United States and Canada on one side and to the rivers of Alaska and eastern Asia on the other.

DISCOVERY FACT™

The adult salmon's journey back to the river where it was born takes an estimated three months.

1 Strenuous Race
Salmon swim upstream from the ocean to the river. On the way, many fall prey to bears.

Neither waterfalls nor strong currents can stop salmon in their journey.

6 Death
Adult salmon die a few days after spawning, exhausted by the work they have done. Their bodies decompose along the riverbank.

5 Fry
Only 40 percent of the eggs laid each fall hatch. The fry remain in the river for up to two years and then migrate to the ocean.

2 Red River

The salmon returns to its birthplace to spawn. Males have intense coloration with a green head.

Seen from above, salmon appear as a large red spot.

Survival

Of the more than 7,500 eggs that two females might lay, only two hatched fish will remain at the end of the life cycle of two years. Many eggs die before hatching, and after hatching, salmon fry are easy prey for other fish.

EGGS		7,500
FRY		4,500
FRY		650
FRY		200
SALMON		50
ADULT SALMON		4
EGG SPAWNING		2

6-Year Cycle

FROM SPAWNING TO ADULTHOOD.

3 The Couple

While females are busy preparing nests in the sand to deposit their eggs, males compete for mates.

BACK
A hump develops in the dorsal section of the body.

5,000
THE QUANTITY OF EGGS A FEMALE CAN LAY.

MOUTH
During the mating season, the lower jaw of the male curves upward.

COLOR
The blue-backed salmon turns a fiery red.

4 Spawning

The female deposits between 2,500 and 5,000 eggs in a series of nests. The male fertilizes them as they fall between the rocks.

Kings of Darkness

In depths below 8,200 feet (2,500 m), where barely any light penetrates, live rare species known as abyssal fish. In this environment, life is possible near hydrothermal vents in the seafloor that warm the nearby waters. In spite of this natural warmth, in many areas the temperature never rises above 36°F (2°C). At this depth, fish have peculiar shapes, with large heads and strong teeth for eating other fish, because no vegetation can grow there. To attract their prey, many have "lure" organs made of photophores that shine in the darkness. The fish are usually black or dark brown for purposes of camouflage.

8,200 feet
(2,500 m) DEPTH OF WATER.

FANFIN SEADEVIL
Caulophryne jordani
This dark-brown fish uses the photophore organ on its head to penetrate the darkness.

SLOANE'S VIPERFISH
Chauliodus sloani
Between 12 and 20 inches (30–50 cm) long, it is dark blue or silvery in color and lives in warm tropical waters.

SHARP, POINTED TEETH
It gulps down its prey after grabbing them with its enormous teeth and its strong suction force.

LANTERN
Like most abyssal fish, it has a lure organ.

EYES FOR SEEING IN DIM LIGHT

TAPETUM
reflects light like a mirror. Each ray hits the retina twice, doubling its sensitivity.

RAY OF LIGHT

RETINA
Blind to red light. It registers only blue light waves, which travel better in the water.

FANGTOOTH
Anoplogaster cornuta
This fearsome hunter kills its prey by seizing it with its jaw and strong teeth.

FILAMENTS
cover its entire body for protection.

FUMAROLE
Openings in the Earth's surface that discharge geothermal water and minerals. As the water cools, these minerals solidify.

36°F
(2°C)
TEMPERATURE OF WATER HEATED BY FUMAROLES.

TUBE-WORM TENTACLES
Tube worms have neither mouths nor digestive tracts. They feed on organic molecules formed from elements in the water by chemosynthetic bacteria that live inside the worms.

DRAGONFISH
Bathophilus sp.
Found in most tropical regions of the world, it has photophores along both sides of its body.

CHIN APPENDAGE shines in the darkness.

LANTERN produces bluish light, which reaches farthest underwater.

1.3 cubic yards (1 cu m) of water = 1.1 tons (1,000 kg)

HYDROSTATIC PRESSURE
The weight of a column of water. The weight of the water increases the pressure of the water with depth. In the Mariana Trench (the deepest undersea trench on the planet), every square inch bears the weight of 7¼ tons (1.1 tonnes per sq cm) of water.

SKIN
Dark colors are likely to make it invisible to attackers.

HUMPBACK ANGLERFISH
Melanocetus johnsonii
6 inches (15 cm) long. Its small fins are insufficient to enable fast maneuvering.

DIMENSIONS

Weight 10½ ounces (300 g)
4 inches (10 cm)

GLOWING LURE produces light to attract prey.

KILLER JAWS
In the ocean's depths, only the best hunter survives.

CHIN APPENDAGE produces light to attract prey.

ILLUMINATED NETDEVIL
Linophryne arborifera
has a glowing lure on the end of its nose and a branching beard that also glows to attract prey. The male is smaller than the female and lives off her like a parasite.

TAILS AND FINS contain luminous cells.

GLOWING LURE gives off light to attract prey.

ATLANTIC FOOTBALL FISH
Himantolophus groenlandicus
The females can reach up to 24 inches (60 cm) long, whereas the males barely reach 1½ inches (4 cm) long and live as parasites on their mates.

Between Land and Water

As indicated by their name (amphi, "both," and bios, "life"), amphibians lead a double existence. When young, they live in the water, and when they become adults they live outside it. In any case, many must remain near water or in very humid places to keep from drying out. This is because these animals also breathe through their skin, and only moist skin can absorb oxygen. Some typical characteristics of adult frogs and toads include a tailless body, long hind limbs, and large eyes that often bulge.

Amphibian Anatomy

Their anatomy has several peculiarities. Larvae, such as tadpoles, have a respiratory system with gills. Most species develop lungs when they reach adulthood. They also have a trachea, pharynx, and saclike lungs, even though skin breathing is at times more important than lung breathing. The heart has two auricles and one ventricle, and the digestive and excretory systems are similar to those of mammals.

The Skin

Amphibians breathe through their skin, which is clean and smooth, without hair or scales. They must always keep it moist, because it has a strong tendency to dry out. Even though they have mucous glands that help maintain moisture, amphibians must live in damp places. The skin of most amphibians protects them from possible predators and has poisonous glands that secrete unpleasant and even toxic substances.

VOCAL SACS

Both toads and frogs sing. The sound is originally produced by their vocal cords, but in males it is amplified by means of inflatable sacs on each side of the larynx.

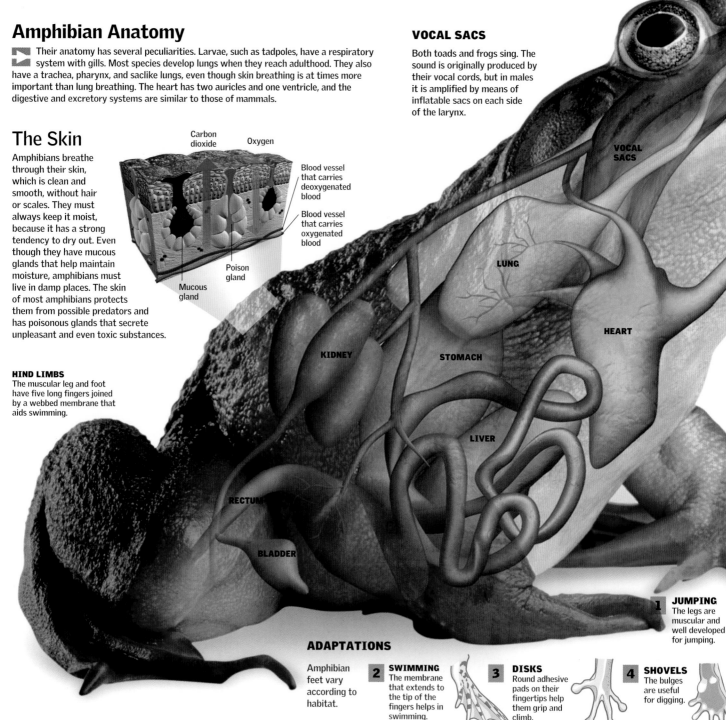

Carbon dioxide

Oxygen

Blood vessel that carries deoxygenated blood

Blood vessel that carries oxygenated blood

Poison gland

Mucous gland

VOCAL SACS

LUNG

HEART

KIDNEY

STOMACH

LIVER

RECTUM

BLADDER

HIND LIMBS
The muscular leg and foot have five long fingers joined by a webbed membrane that aids swimming.

ADAPTATIONS

Amphibian feet vary according to habitat.

1 JUMPING
The legs are muscular and well developed for jumping.

2 SWIMMING
The membrane that extends to the tip of the fingers helps in swimming.

3 DISKS
Round adhesive pads on their fingertips help them grip and climb.

4 SHOVELS
The bulges are useful for digging.

Differences Between Frogs and Toads

Because of their similar shape, frogs and toads are often confused, but they are actually quite different animals. Toads have wrinkled skin and short legs, and they are land animals. Frogs are smaller, have webbed feet, and live in the water and in trees.

SKIN
Soft and smooth, with strong, bright colors

EYES
Frogs have horizontal pupils.

EYES
The pupil is usually horizontal, although some toads have vertical pupils.

SKIN
The skin of a toad is wrinkled, hard, rough, and dry. It is sometimes used as leather.

COMMON TOAD
Bufo bufo

REED FROG
Hyperolius tuberilinguis

POSTURE
Toads are terrestrial species, slow-moving, and wider than frogs. Frogs live mainly in water, which is why they have webbed toes adapted for swimming.

LEGS
are long and are adapted for jumping. Frogs have webbed toes to help with swimming.

LEGS
are shorter and wider than those of frogs and are adapted for walking.

CATCHING PREY
Toads gulp down their prey, swallowing it whole.

SWALLOWING
Eye retraction, where the toad closes and turns its eyes inward, increases the pressure in the mouth, pushing food down the esophagus.

Nutrition

During the larval stage, nutrition is based on plants, whereas in the adult stage the main food sources are arthropods (such as beetles and spiders) and other invertebrates, such as butterfly caterpillars and earthworms.

Types of Amphibians

Amphibians are divided into three groups that are differentiated on the basis of tail and legs. Newts and salamanders have tails. They belong to the order Urodela. Frogs and toads, which have no tail except as tadpoles, belong to the Anura group. Caecilians, which have no tail or legs, are similar to worms and belong to the Apoda group.

1
ANURA
Tailless

EUROPEAN TREE FROG
Hyla arborea
A small docile species that lives near buildings.

2
APODA
Without legs

RINGED CAECILIAN
Siphonops annulatus
Resembles a large, thick worm.

3
URODELA
With a tail

TIGER SALAMANDER
Ambystoma tigrinum
One of the most colorful in North America.

Legs

Frogs and toads have four fingers on each front leg and five on each hind leg. Water frogs have webbed feet; tree frogs have adhesive disks on the tips of their fingers to hold on to vertical surfaces; and burrowing frogs have callous protuberances (called "tubercules") on their hind legs, which they use for digging.

Metamorphosis

Metamorphosis is the process of transformation experienced by anurans (it can also be observed in amphibians from the order Urodela and caecilians), starting with the egg and ending at the adult stage. Amphibians leave the egg in a larval form. They then undergo very important changes in their anatomy, diet, and lifestyle, slowly mutating from their first stage, which is completely aquatic, until they transform into animals adapted to life on land.

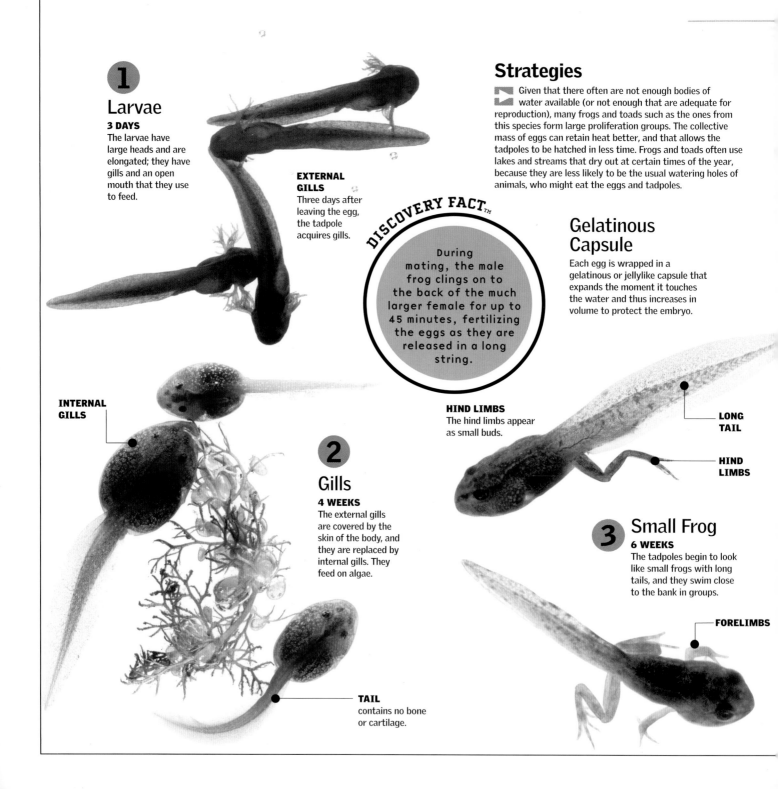

1 Larvae
3 DAYS
The larvae have large heads and are elongated; they have gills and an open mouth that they use to feed.

EXTERNAL GILLS
Three days after leaving the egg, the tadpole acquires gills.

INTERNAL GILLS

2 Gills
4 WEEKS
The external gills are covered by the skin of the body, and they are replaced by internal gills. They feed on algae.

TAIL
contains no bone or cartilage.

Strategies
Given that there often are not enough bodies of water available (or not enough that are adequate for reproduction), many frogs and toads such as the ones from this species form large proliferation groups. The collective mass of eggs can retain heat better, and that allows the tadpoles to be hatched in less time. Frogs and toads often use lakes and streams that dry out at certain times of the year, because they are less likely to be the usual watering holes of animals, who might eat the eggs and tadpoles.

DISCOVERY FACT™
During mating, the male frog clings on to the back of the much larger female for up to 45 minutes, fertilizing the eggs as they are released in a long string.

Gelatinous Capsule
Each egg is wrapped in a gelatinous or jellylike capsule that expands the moment it touches the water and thus increases in volume to protect the embryo.

HIND LIMBS
The hind limbs appear as small buds.

LONG TAIL

HIND LIMBS

3 Small Frog
6 WEEKS
The tadpoles begin to look like small frogs with long tails, and they swim close to the bank in groups.

FORELIMBS

Cycle
METAMORPHOSIS

The development of the common European frog from egg to adult takes approximately 16 weeks.

Mother Frog and Her Eggs

Despite the fact that the survival instinct of anurans is not fully developed, frogs and toads somehow take care of their future young. Laying eggs in great quantities ensures that many tadpoles will be able to escape predators who feed on the eggs. The gelatinous layer also protects the eggs from other predators. Some frogs even care for their tadpoles by nestling them on their backs. An example of such a frog is the Surinam toad.

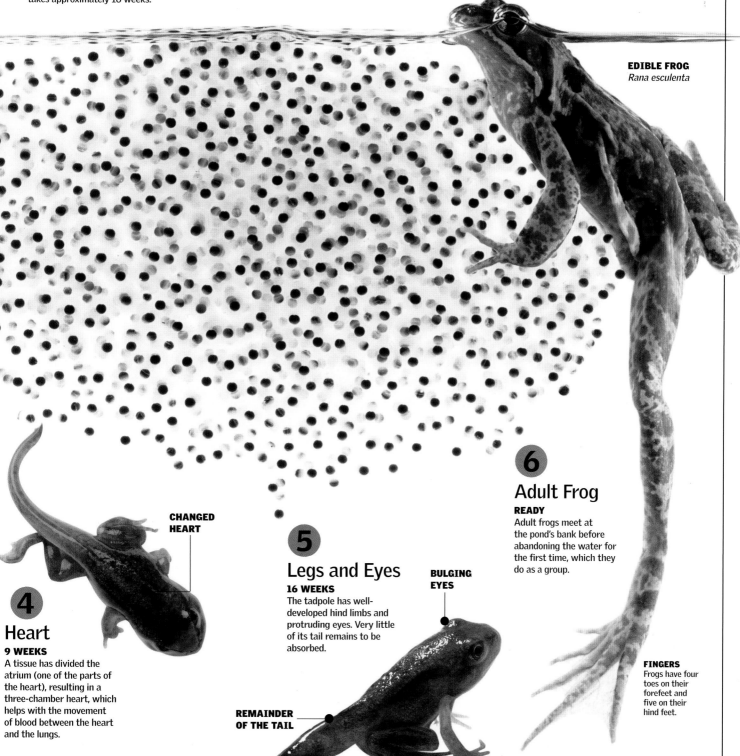

EDIBLE FROG
Rana esculenta

CHANGED HEART

6

Adult Frog

READY
Adult frogs meet at the pond's bank before abandoning the water for the first time, which they do as a group.

5

Legs and Eyes

16 WEEKS
The tadpole has well-developed hind limbs and protruding eyes. Very little of its tail remains to be absorbed.

BULGING EYES

4

Heart

9 WEEKS
A tissue has divided the atrium (one of the parts of the heart), resulting in a three-chamber heart, which helps with the movement of blood between the heart and the lungs.

REMAINDER OF THE TAIL

FINGERS
Frogs have four toes on their forefeet and five on their hind feet.

Jointless

The body of most mollusks is soft, extremely flexible, and without joints, but many have a large, hard shell. Most species live in the ocean, but they are also found in lakes and land environments. All modern mollusks have bilateral symmetry, one cephalopod foot with sensory organs and locomotion, a visceral mass, and a covering, the mantle, that secretes the shell. They feed by means of a unique rasplike mouth structure called a radula.

INTESTINE

GONAD

DIGESTIVE GLAND

LUNG

Gastropods

These mollusks are characterized by their large ventral foot, whose wavelike motions are used to move from place to place. The group comprises snails and slugs, and they can live on land, in the ocean, and in freshwater. When these animals have a shell, it is a single spiral-shaped piece, and the extreme flexibility of the rest of the body allows the gastropod to draw itself up completely within the shell. Gastropods have eyes and one or two pairs of tentacles on their head.

KIDNEY   HEART

PROSOBRANCHIA

This mollusk subclass mainly includes marine animals. Some have mother-of-pearl on the inside of their shell, whereas others have a substance similar to porcelain.

SALIVARY GLAND

ESOPHAGUS

FEMALE SEXUAL ORGAN

LUNGED

Snails, land slugs, and freshwater slugs have lungs, and their lung sacs allow them to breathe oxygen in the atmosphere.

OPISTHOBRANCHIA

are sea slugs, which are characterized by having a very small shell or no shell at all.

BENDING OF THE SNAIL

In snails, bending is a phenomenon that moves the cavity of the mantle from the rear toward the front of the body. The visceral organs rotate 180 degrees, and the digestive tube and the nervous connections cross in a figure of eight.

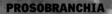

Gills

Nervous system

Digestive tract

SEA ANGEL
Candida sp.

Bivalves

Mollusks with a shell divided into two halves. The two parts of the shell are joined by an elastic ligament that opens the shell, abductor muscles that close the shell, and the umbo, a system of ridges that helps the shell shut tightly. Almost all bivalves feed on microorganisms. Some bury themselves in wet sand, digging small tunnels that let in water and food. The tunnels can be from a fraction of an inch long to over a yard long.

SCALLOP
Pecten jacobaeus

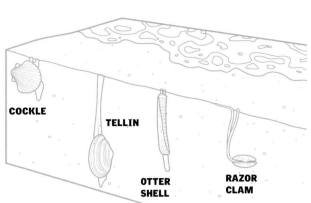

COCKLE

TELLIN

OTTER SHELL

RAZOR CLAM

Under the Sand

Many mollusks live buried under the sand in order to hide from predators and the effects of waves, wind, and sudden changes in temperature.

100,000

THE NUMBER OF LIVING MOLLUSK SPECIES; AS MANY MORE HAVE BECOME EXTINCT.

LAMELLIBRANCHIATA

Include most bivalves. They use gills to breathe and to feed. They have no differentiated head, eyes, or extremities. They can grow up to 5 inches (13 cm) long, and they rest on the ocean floor.

GREEN MUSSEL
Perna viridis

PROTOBRANCHIA

This class includes bivalves with a split lower foot, called a "sole." Bivalves use their gills only to breathe. This subclass includes small bivalves ½ inch (13 mm) wide, called nutclams (*Nucula nitidosa*).

BROWN GARDEN SNAIL
Helix aspersa

RADULA

Cephalopods

Cuttlefish, octopus, squid, and nautilus are called cephalopods because their extremities, or tentacles, are attached directly to their heads. These predators are adapted to life in the oceans, and they have quite complex nervous, sensory, and motion systems. Their tentacles surround their mouths, which have a radula and a powerful beak. Cephalopods range from ⅓ inch (1 cm) to several yards long.

NAUTILUS
Nautilus sp.

COLEOIDEA

Cephalopods of this class have a very small internal shell, or none at all, and only two gills. Except for the nautilus, this class includes all cephalopods alive today—octopus, cuttlefish, and squid.

NAUTILOIDEA

This subclass populated the oceans of the Paleozoic and Mesozoic periods, but today only one genus—*Nautilus*—survives. A nautilus has an outer shell, four gills, and ten tentacles. Its shell is made from calcium, is spiral in shape, and is divided into chambers.

COMMON CUTTLEFISH
Sepia officinalis

Colorful Armor

Even though they inhabit all known environments, crustaceans are most closely identified with the aquatic environment. That is where they were transformed into arthropods with the most evolutionary success. Their bodies are divided into three parts: the cephalothorax, with antennae and strong mandibles; the abdomen, or pleon; and the back (telson). Some crustaceans are very small: sea lice, for instance, are no larger than $\frac{1}{100}$ inch (0.25 mm). The Japanese spider crab, on the other hand, is more than 9 feet (3 m) long with outstretched legs, because it has legs in both its abdomen and its thorax, in addition to two pairs of antennae.

WOOD LOUSE

Armadillidium vulgare
This invertebrate, belonging to the order Isopoda, is one of the few terrestrial crustaceans, and it is probably the one best adapted to life out of water. When it feels threatened, it rolls itself up, leaving only its exoskeleton exposed. Even though it can reproduce and develop away from water, it breathes through gills. The gills are found in its abdominal appendages and for this reason must be kept at specific humidity levels. That is also why the wood louse seeks dark and humid environments, such as under rocks, on dead or fallen leaves, and in fallen tree trunks.

Extended animal

EXOSKELETON
Divided into independent parts

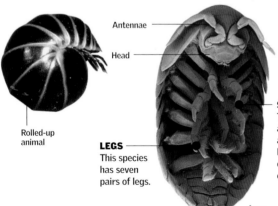

Antennae

Head

Rolled-up animal

LEGS
This species has seven pairs of legs.

SEGMENTS
The back segments are smaller, and when they bend, they help enclose the animal completely.

Anus

Malacostraca

is the name given to the class of crustaceans that groups crabs together with sea lobsters, shrimp, wood lice, and sea lice. The term comes from Greek, and means "soft-shelled." Sea and river crabs have ten legs, and one pair of these legs is modified in a pincer form. Malacostraca are omnivorous and have adapted to a great variety of environments; the number of segments of their exoskeleton varies from a minimum of 16 to more than 60.

APPENDAGES
consist of a lower region from which two segmented branches grow, one internal (endopod) and the other external (exopod).

THE PACIFIC SPIDER
CRAB CAN WEIGH UP TO

45 pounds
(20 kg).

BARNACLES WITHOUT A SHELL

BARNACLE COLONY

Together Forever

At birth, barnacles (*Pollicipes cornucopia*) are microscopic larvae that travel through the sea until they reach a rocky coast. There they attach themselves to the shore by means of a stalk, which they develop by the modification of their antennae, and then form a shell. Once they are attached, they remain in one spot for the rest of their lives, absorbing food from the water. Barnacles are edible.

BARNACLE TRANSVERSAL CUT

SEGMENTED LEGS

MOUTH

SOFT AREA

SHELL

LEGS EXTENDED TO CATCH FOOD

SHELL

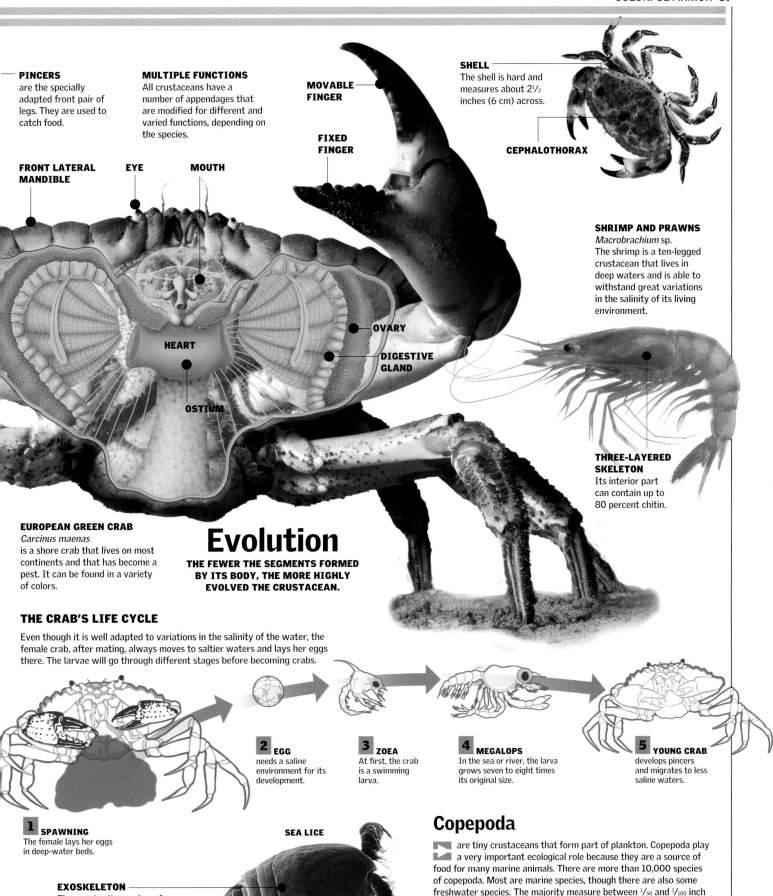

PINCERS
are the specially adapted front pair of legs. They are used to catch food.

MULTIPLE FUNCTIONS
All crustaceans have a number of appendages that are modified for different and varied functions, depending on the species.

MOVABLE FINGER

FIXED FINGER

SHELL
The shell is hard and measures about 2½ inches (6 cm) across.

CEPHALOTHORAX

FRONT LATERAL MANDIBLE

EYE

MOUTH

OVARY

DIGESTIVE GLAND

HEART

OSTIUM

SHRIMP AND PRAWNS
Macrobrachium sp.
The shrimp is a ten-legged crustacean that lives in deep waters and is able to withstand great variations in the salinity of its living environment.

THREE-LAYERED SKELETON
Its interior part can contain up to 80 percent chitin.

EUROPEAN GREEN CRAB
Carcinus maenas
is a shore crab that lives on most continents and that has become a pest. It can be found in a variety of colors.

Evolution
THE FEWER THE SEGMENTS FORMED BY ITS BODY, THE MORE HIGHLY EVOLVED THE CRUSTACEAN.

THE CRAB'S LIFE CYCLE

Even though it is well adapted to variations in the salinity of the water, the female crab, after mating, always moves to saltier waters and lays her eggs there. The larvae will go through different stages before becoming crabs.

2 EGG
needs a saline environment for its development.

3 ZOEA
At first, the crab is a swimming larva.

4 MEGALOPS
In the sea or river, the larva grows seven to eight times its original size.

5 YOUNG CRAB
develops pincers and migrates to less saline waters.

1 SPAWNING
The female lays her eggs in deep-water beds.

SEA LICE

EXOSKELETON
The greater its number of segments, the less highly evolved the species.

Copepoda

are tiny crustaceans that form part of plankton. Copepoda play a very important ecological role because they are a source of food for many marine animals. There are more than 10,000 species of copepoda. Most are marine species, though there are also some freshwater species. The majority measure between $\frac{1}{50}$ and $\frac{1}{100}$ inch (0.5–2 mm) long; the smallest ones (*Sphaeronellopsis monothrix*) reach only $\frac{1}{250}$ inch (0.11 mm) in length, and the largest (*Pennella balaenopterae*) are 13 inches (32 cm) long.

Eight Legs

Arachnids make up the largest and most important class of Chelicerata. Among them are spiders, scorpions, fleas, ticks, and mites. Arachnids were the first arthropods to migrate from the oceans and colonize terrestrial environments, and nearly all species now live on land. The best-known arachnids are the scorpions and spiders, both found on every continent except Antarctica.

The female can transport up to 30 offspring on her back.

GIANT HOUSEHOLD SPIDER
Tegenaria duellica
This spider is distinguished by its long legs in relation to its body.

DISCOVERY FACT™

Fossil scorpions dating from the Silurian period, 430 million years ago, show that these animals have changed little in form and behavior.

Scorpions

Long feared by people, the scorpion is characterized by the fact that its chelicerae (mouth parts that are large in scorpions) and pedipalps form pincers. The body is covered with a chitinous exoskeleton that includes the cephalothorax and abdomen.

EMPEROR SCORPION
Pandinus imperator
Like other scorpions, it has a stinger crisscrossed by venomous glands. It measures between 5 and 7 inches (12–18 cm) long, although some have reached a length of 8 inches (20 cm).

The claws hold the prey and immobilize it.

PEDIPALPS
The terminal pedipalp forms a copulating organ through which the male inseminates the female.

PEDIPALPS
act as sensory organs and manipulate food. Males also use them for copulation.

CHELICERAE
move up and down and are used as sensors. In the more primitive spiders (such as tarantulas), they move from side to side like pincers.

SALIVA GLANDS

TICK

Visible dorsal capitulum with projections that can easily be detached from the tick.

MIDDLE STOMACH

PALPS

ADHESION MATERIAL

INFECTION

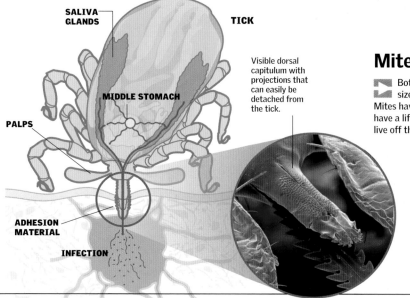

Mites and Ticks

Both are members of the Acari order and are chiefly differentiated by their size. Mites are smaller; ticks may measure up to 1 inch (2.5 cm) in length. Mites have many diverse forms and are parasites of animals and plants. Most ticks have a life cycle of three stages: larva, nymph, and adult, during each of which they live off the blood of their hosts and are vectors of a number of infectious diseases.

TICK Palps

MITE Palps

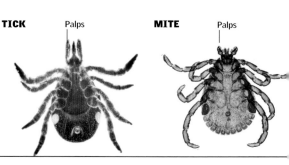

100,000

S THE NUMBER OF SPECIES OF RACHNIDS THOUGHT TO EXIST N THE WORLD.

EXOSKELETON
Growth happens through molting, a process by which the spider gets rid of its old exoskeleton. In its youth the spider grows through successive moltings (up to four a year), and once it reaches adulthood, it goes through a yearly change.

1 The front edge of the shell comes off, and the tegument separates from the abdomen.

2 The spider raises and lowers its legs until the skin slips off.

3 It discards the old exoskeleton, and the new one hardens on contact with the air.

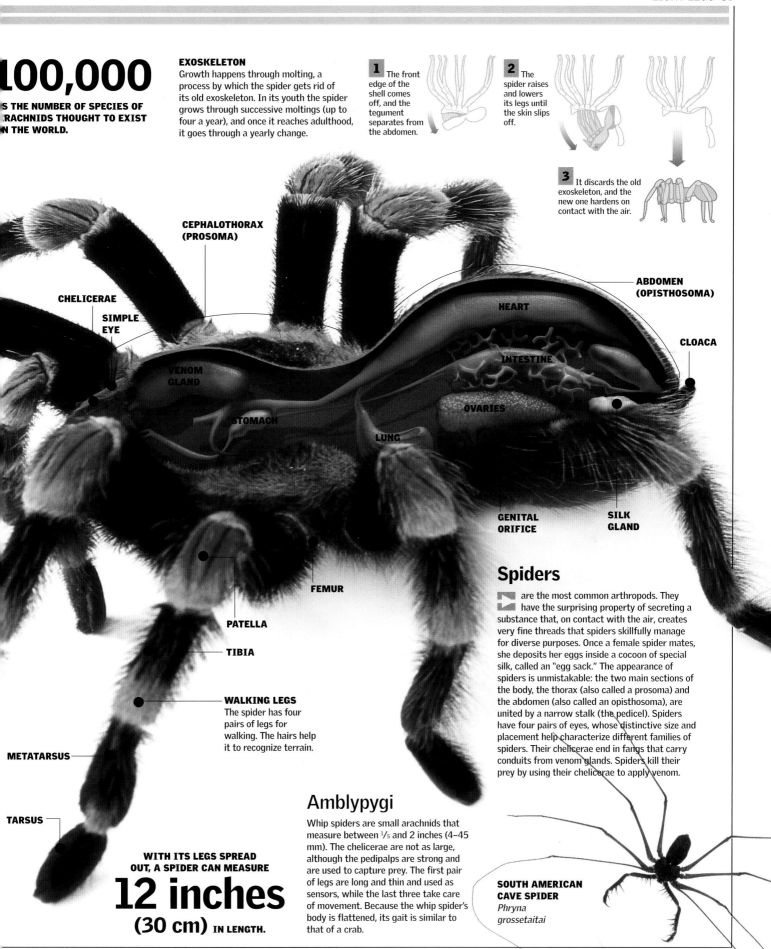

CEPHALOTHORAX (PROSOMA)

CHELICERAE

SIMPLE EYE

VENOM GLAND

STOMACH

LUNG

ABDOMEN (OPISTHOSOMA)

HEART

INTESTINE

CLOACA

OVARIES

GENITAL ORIFICE

SILK GLAND

FEMUR

PATELLA

TIBIA

WALKING LEGS
The spider has four pairs of legs for walking. The hairs help it to recognize terrain.

METATARSUS

TARSUS

WITH ITS LEGS SPREAD OUT, A SPIDER CAN MEASURE

12 inches
(30 cm) IN LENGTH.

Spiders

are the most common arthropods. They have the surprising property of secreting a substance that, on contact with the air, creates very fine threads that spiders skillfully manage for diverse purposes. Once a female spider mates, she deposits her eggs inside a cocoon of special silk, called an "egg sack." The appearance of spiders is unmistakable: the two main sections of the body, the thorax (also called a prosoma) and the abdomen (also called an opisthosoma), are united by a narrow stalk (the pedicel). Spiders have four pairs of eyes, whose distinctive size and placement help characterize different families of spiders. Their chelicerae end in fangs that carry conduits from venom glands. Spiders kill their prey by using their chelicerae to apply venom.

Amblypygi

Whip spiders are small arachnids that measure between 1/5 and 2 inches (4–45 mm). The chelicerae are not as large, although the pedipalps are strong and are used to capture prey. The first pair of legs are long and thin and used as sensors, while the last three take care of movement. Because the whip spider's body is flattened, its gait is similar to that of a crab.

SOUTH AMERICAN CAVE SPIDER
Phryna grossetaitai

Secrets of Success

Sensory antennae, highly developed eyes on the sides of the head, and pairs of jointed legs with functions that depend on the species—all are outstanding features of insects and myriapods. Insects, also called hexapods, have six legs attached to the thorax. Myriapods (millipedes and centipedes) are multisegmented arthropods that have developed only on land.

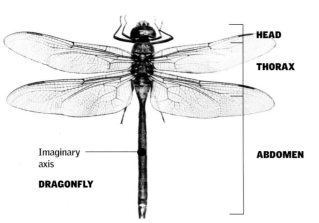

HEAD

THORAX

ABDOMEN

Imaginary axis

DRAGONFLY

BILATERAL SYMMETRY

The entire body of insects and myriapods is composed of pairs, arranged along an imaginary axis that passes from the head to the lower end of the abdomen.

Two Pairs of Wings

Some ancient species had three pairs of wings. Today, however, insects have one or two pairs. Butterflies, dragonflies, bees, and wasps use two pairs to fly, but other insects fly with only one pair.

OPEN CIRCULATION

A tubular heart pumps the hemolymph (blood) through the dorsal aorta. Accessory contracting organs help push the blood into the wings and legs.

HIND WINGS

AT REST
Dragonflies can place their wings against their bodies.

APPENDAGE
contains the genital organs.

SEGMENTED REGIONS

Insects' bodies are divided into three parts: the head (6 segments), the thorax (3 segments), and the abdomen (up to 11 segments).

SPIRACLES
Small entrances to the tracheae.

1 million
KNOWN INSECT SPECIES

RESPIRATORY SYSTEM

Land-dwelling arthropods breathe with tracheae. Through branching tubes (tracheoles), air containing oxygen is brought directly to each cell, and carbon dioxide is eliminated.

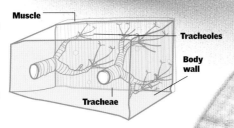

Muscle

Tracheoles

Body wall

Tracheae

Legs Adapted for Type of Use

The shape of the arthropod legs shown here is closely related to their use and to the arthropod's habitat. Some species have taste and touch receptors on their legs.

Sacs

STRUCTURE
gives the wings great stability.

LEGS

WALKING	JUMPING	SWIMMING	DIGGING	GATHERING
Cockroach	Grasshopper	Water scorpion	Mole cricket	Bee

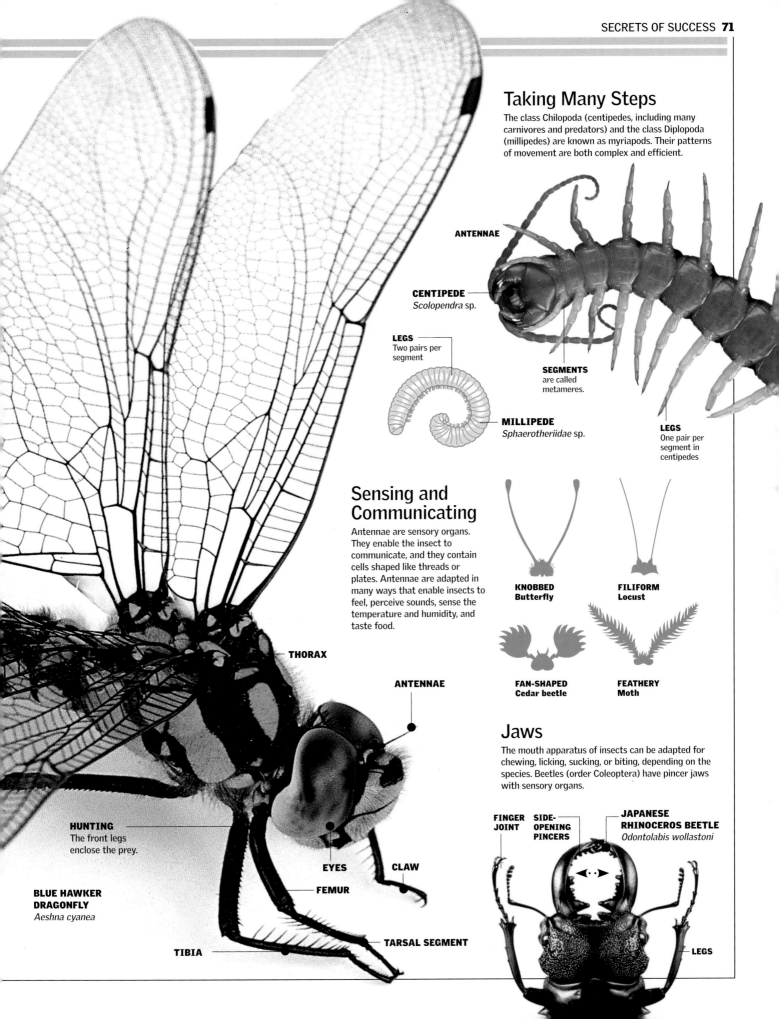

Taking Many Steps

The class Chilopoda (centipedes, including many carnivores and predators) and the class Diplopoda (millipedes) are known as myriapods. Their patterns of movement are both complex and efficient.

ANTENNAE

CENTIPEDE
Scolopendra sp.

LEGS
Two pairs per segment

SEGMENTS
are called metameres.

MILLIPEDE
Sphaerotheriidae sp.

LEGS
One pair per segment in centipedes

Sensing and Communicating

Antennae are sensory organs. They enable the insect to communicate, and they contain cells shaped like threads or plates. Antennae are adapted in many ways that enable insects to feel, perceive sounds, sense the temperature and humidity, and taste food.

KNOBBED
Butterfly

FILIFORM
Locust

FAN-SHAPED
Cedar beetle

FEATHERY
Moth

THORAX

ANTENNAE

Jaws

The mouth apparatus of insects can be adapted for chewing, licking, sucking, or biting, depending on the species. Beetles (order Coleoptera) have pincer jaws with sensory organs.

HUNTING
The front legs enclose the prey.

FINGER JOINT

SIDE-OPENING PINCERS

JAPANESE RHINOCEROS BEETLE
Odontolabis wollastoni

BLUE HAWKER DRAGONFLY
Aeshna cyanea

EYES

CLAW

FEMUR

TIBIA

TARSAL SEGMENT

LEGS

The Art of Flying

One of the most basic adaptations of insects has been their ability to fly. Most have two pairs of wings. Beetles (order Coleoptera) use one pair to fly and one pair for protection. For example, the rounded body of a ladybug is nothing more than the covering for a very sophisticated flight system. It makes these small beetles, which are harmless to humans, great hunters in the insect world.

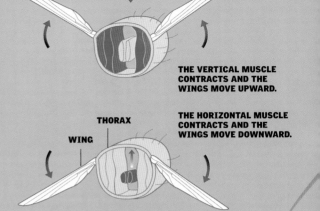

THE VERTICAL MUSCLE CONTRACTS AND THE WINGS MOVE UPWARD.

THORAX

WING

THE HORIZONTAL MUSCLE CONTRACTS AND THE WINGS MOVE DOWNWARD.

"Ladies" of Land and Air

Some 4,500 species of these beetles live throughout the world. Almost all are brightly colored, with black spots on a red, yellow, or orange background. These colors warn off predators, who usually associate bright colors with poison. In fact, some ladybugs are actually poisonous for small predators, such as lizards and small birds. Ladybugs pose the greatest danger to agricultural pests, such as plant lice and gadflies, so they are often used as a natural biological pest control.

3

Flight

With the elytra open and spread like airplane wings, the second pair of wings is free to move. The muscles at their base control the direction of flight.

2

Takeoff

Although the colorful elytra are not used in flying, the insect needs to lift them in order to unfold its wings, which are seen only during flight.

FRONT VIEW OF ELYTRA

Raised elytra

40–80 inches
per second
(1–2 m/s)

IS THE AVERAGE SPEED OF FLIGHT.

SEVEN-SPOTTED LADYBUG
Coccinella septempunctata
Thanks to their help in destroying pests, during the Middle Ages these beetles were considered instruments of divine intervention from the Virgin Mary, so were known as "Our Lady's bird."

The insect is between $1/25$ and $1/2$ inch (0.1–1 cm) long.

1

Preparation

The elytra, or modified front wings, can separate from the rest of the body. They protect the thorax, and also the wings when folded inside.

WINGS PREPARED FOR FLIGHT

BACK VIEW

RAISED ELYTRON

VISIBLE WING

APOSEMATISM
The opposite of mimetism: These insects use their bright colors to scare away danger.

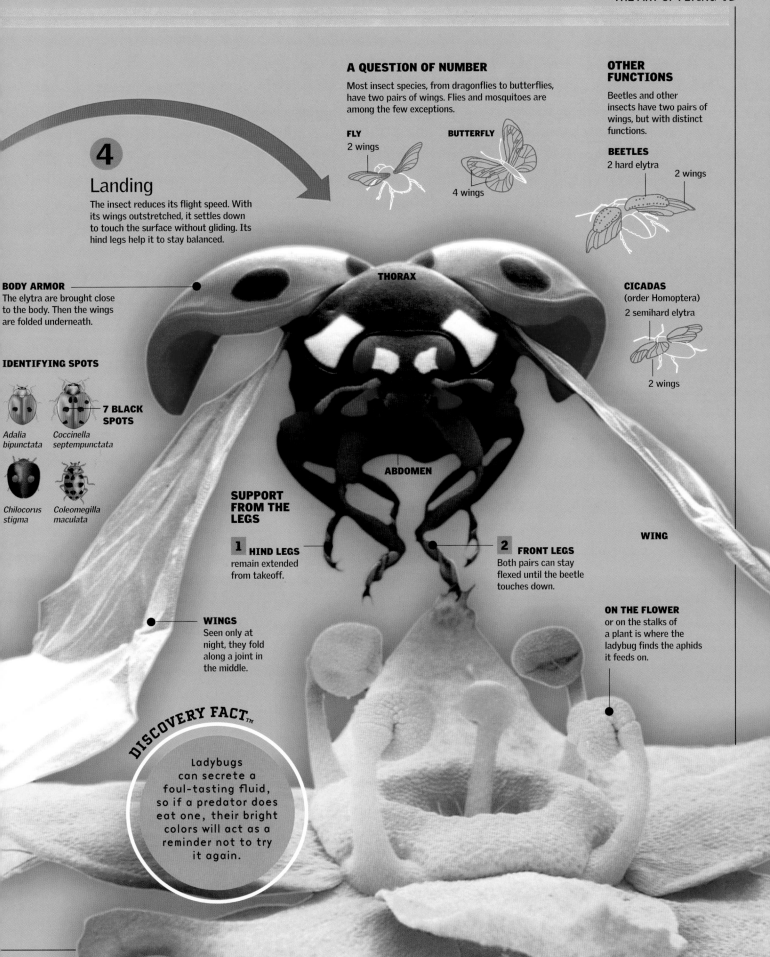

A QUESTION OF NUMBER

Most insect species, from dragonflies to butterflies, have two pairs of wings. Flies and mosquitoes are among the few exceptions.

FLY
2 wings

BUTTERFLY
4 wings

OTHER FUNCTIONS

Beetles and other insects have two pairs of wings, but with distinct functions.

BEETLES
2 hard elytra
2 wings

CICADAS
(order Homoptera)
2 semihard elytra
2 wings

4
Landing

The insect reduces its flight speed. With its wings outstretched, it settles down to touch the surface without gliding. Its hind legs help it to stay balanced.

BODY ARMOR
The elytra are brought close to the body. Then the wings are folded underneath.

THORAX

IDENTIFYING SPOTS

7 BLACK SPOTS

Adalia bipunctata

Coccinella septempunctata

Chilocorus stigma

Coleomegilla maculata

ABDOMEN

SUPPORT FROM THE LEGS

1 **HIND LEGS** remain extended from takeoff.

2 **FRONT LEGS**
Both pairs can stay flexed until the beetle touches down.

WING

WINGS
Seen only at night, they fold along a joint in the middle.

ON THE FLOWER
or on the stalks of a plant is where the ladybug finds the aphids it feeds on.

DISCOVERY FACT™

Ladybugs can secrete a foul-tasting fluid, so if a predator does eat one, their bright colors will act as a reminder not to try it again.

Order and Progress

Ants are one of the insects with the highest social organization. In the anthill, each inhabitant has a job to do. The head of the family is the queen, the only one that reproduces. All the rest of the ants are her offspring. During mating, queens and drones (males) from various colonies mate on the wing. The queens need to mate several times, because the sperm they receive will have to last their lifetime. There are about 10,000 different ant species.

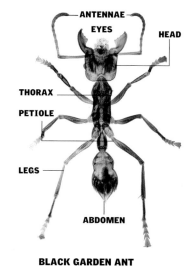

ANTENNAE
EYES
HEAD
THORAX
PETIOLE
LEGS
ABDOMEN

BLACK GARDEN ANT
Lasius niger

MAIN
ENTRANCE

The Anthill

After mating, the queen loses her wings and chooses a place to lay eggs. At first she lives on reserves derived from the muscle mass of her wings and some of the first eggs she has laid. She takes charge of raising the first generation of worker ants, which will then take on the task of finding food while the queen focuses exclusively on laying eggs.

COMMUNICATION

An ant communicates with its antennae through chemical means, by capturing particles of certain substances (pheromones) that enable it to recognize another ant from the same colony. Ants do not have a well-developed sense for perceiving sound.

FOOD STORAGE
Honeypot ants coordinate the food supply.

METAMORPHOSIS

In the egg stage, the future ant remains near the queen but leaves her during the larval stage. Other ants then take care of the larva, until it becomes a nymph and forms a cocoon from which it will emerge as an adult.

EGGS   LARVAE   NYMPHS   COCOON

UNUSED TUNNEL

DISCOVERY FACT™

The total weight of all the ants in the world is roughly equal to the weight of all the humans in the world.

2 LARVAE
are carried to another chamber to grow.

3 NYMPHS
are fed and taken care of in another area.

1 EGGS
are laid by the queen in the lowest area.

4 COCOONS
The new ants hatch ready to work.

QUEEN ANT

YOUNG ANTS

The Castes

Each ant plays a role in the nest and is assigned its role at birth. Drone, soldier, worker, and replete worker (specialized to store food reserves) are the castes that distinguish what chores each ant will have.

Four wings

QUEEN
The largest ant. She lays the eggs that will become workers, drones, and new queens.

Two wings

DRONE
His only function is mating; afterward he dies.

WORKER
The worker ant may have the role of gathering food, cleaning, or protecting the anthill.

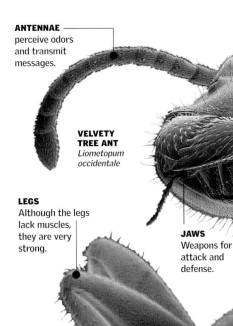

ANTENNAE
perceive odors and transmit messages.

EYES
can see only a few inches.

VELVETY TREE ANT
Liometopum occidentale

LEGS
Although the legs lack muscles, they are very strong.

JAWS
Weapons for attack and defense.

LEGS
Agile and thin.

Feeding

Ants cannot eat solid food. The plants and animals they eat are mixed with saliva to form a paste, which is used to feed the whole colony.

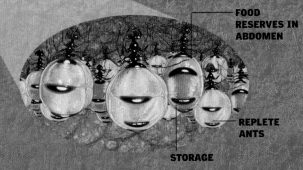

FOOD RESERVES IN ABDOMEN

REPLETE ANTS

STORAGE

INTERCHANGE OF FOOD

Having two stomachs, an ant can share food. The transfer begins when the receiving ant uses its front legs to touch the lip of the donor ant.

CROP
Social pouch

STOMACH
Individual pouch

Defense

The most widely used defense is biting and spraying streams of formic acid. Soldier ants have the job of scaring away the enemy because they have larger heads than worker ants.

JAW

The jaw is the ant's main weapon of defense, with a bite that can scare away or harm a rival. The jaw is also used for hunting and feeding.

AMERICAN FARMER ANT

CLAMPING JAW

VENOM

may contain formic acid and can kill or paralyze the prey. It comes from special glands in the lower abdomen.

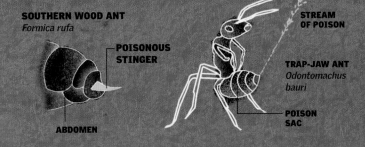

SOUTHERN WOOD ANT
Formica rufa

POISONOUS STINGER

ABDOMEN

STREAM OF POISON

TRAP-JAW ANT
Odontomachus bauri

POISON SAC

Survival Strategies

Evolution has molded some striking traits into living beings. In particular, some insects, disguised as branches or leaves, can escape notice so they can hunt or hide from predators. To avoid being attacked, other insects develop colors and shapes that deceive other animals and put them off attacking. Hiding and showing off are two opposite strategies that have been favoring the survival of the fittest for millions of years.

BRIMSTONE BUTTERFLY
Gonepteryx sp.
The profile of the wings resembles the shape of cut leaves.

PEACOCK BUTTERFLY
Inachis io
The flashy, aposematic (warning) coloration keeps predators away by warning of the danger the insect poses.

WINGS
These wings look like leaves, with a similar color, shape, and structure.

Masters of Simulation

Camouflage, or crypsis, is a phenomenon in which animals use amazing disguises as advantageous adaptations. Camouflage is used both by hunters and by potential prey. Insects' bodies may be disguised to match soil, rock, or parts of trees, such as bark or leaves. These masking techniques are a convenient way for the insect to fade into the background.

FALSE EYE
The scales are pigmented to look like eyes.

Disguise

Some insects use survival strategies designed to keep predators from seeing them. This disguise is their only means of defense.

DOUBLE PROTECTION
Caligo sp.
Owl butterflies combine Batesian and Müllerian mimicry. Predators may confuse the owl butterfly with leaves, but if a predator succeeds in finding it, the butterfly folds its wings to look like the shape and eyes of an owl. The predator, confused, backs off from attacking.

BODY
The abdomen is shaped like a branch.

LEGS
imitate twigs with dry leaves.

AUSTRALIAN STICK INSECT
Extatosoma sp.
This sticklike insect sways back and forth as if tossed by the wind.

Warning Signals

Mimetism is the imitation of characteristics belonging to dangerous or bad-tasting animals. Replicating the colors and shapes of dangerous animals is known as "Batesian mimicry." On the other hand, if an insect produces foul-smelling substances to disgust the predator, that is called "Müllerian mimicry."

DISCOVERY FACT™

The assassin bug *Acanthaspis petax* kills ants and stacks their corpses on its back, to disguise itself from the spiders who prey on it.

VEINS
In an extraordinary simulation, the veins look like the veins of leaves.

Defense

The most widely imitated insects are ants, bees, and wasps, because they produce toxic substances that can be deadly.

THISTLE MANTIS
Blepharopsis mendica
These mantises use camouflage to hunt unsuspecting insects that get too close to their powerful front legs.

EYES
Compound eyes enable them to monitor the slightest movement.

FRONT LEGS
move slowly so that the prey will not detect them.

GLOSSARY

Adaptation
A structural, physiological, or behavioral trait that allows an organism to live in its environment.

Aerodynamic
Having an appropriate shape to decrease resistance to the air.

Amino Acid
Organic molecule from which proteins are produced.

Amphibians
Group including frogs, toads, and salamanders, in which the young live in water and the adults on land.

Anaerobic
Breathing process that does not require oxygen.

Antennae
A pair of long sensory appendages on the head of many arthropods.

Aorta
Main artery in blood circulation systems. It sends blood to other tissues.

Arthropod
An animal with articulated appendages and a segmented body, covered by an exoskeleton.

Bilateral Symmetry
Corporal form whereby the right and left halves are approximate mirror images of each other.

Biped
Animal that stands upright, walks, or runs using only the two hind limbs.

Bony Fish
Fish with bony skeletons and jaws. They have flexible fins that allow precise control of their movements.

Calcite
A form of the chemical compound calcium carbonate.

Cartilaginous Fish
Fish with skeletons made of cartilage, such as sharks and rays.

Carrion
The remains of dead animals used as food by some birds or other animals.

Caste
A social group that carries out specific tasks, characteristic of ants and bees.

Cephalopod
A class of exclusively marine mollusks with tentacles or legs attached to the head. These appendages have rows of suckers that are used for capturing prey and copulation.

Cephalothorax
The head and thorax combined in one single body segment.

Chelicera
First pair of appendages in crabs, sea spiders, and arachnids, usually in the form of pincers or fangs.

Chitin
Durable polysaccharide that contains nitrogen and is found in the exoskeleton of arthropods or other surface structures of many invertebrates.

Chordate
Animal with a spinal cord, whether throughout its development or only in certain stages.

Cloaca
Open chamber into which the urinary and reproductive ducts empty.

Cochlea
A structure like a coiled spiral tube, located in the inner ear of mammals.

Cocoon
A protective sheath, usually of silk, made by insects to protect themselves during the pupa stage.

Cold-blooded
Organism whose body temperature is mainly controlled by external heat sources.

Colony
A group of animals of the same species that live and work together to survive.

Convolution
Each of the slight folds that mark the surface of the cerebral cortex.

Crustacean
An animal of the arthropod group, with antennae and articulated appendages, that uses gills to breathe and has a body protected by a thick covering.

Crop
Sac that communicates with a bird's esophagus, where food is softened.

Dendrite
The branched elongation of a nerve cell through which it receives stimuli.

Dermis
The inner layer of the skin, located under the epidermis.

Dewlap
Fold of skin hanging below the chin and extending to the chest in some lizards and other tetrapods.

Display
Behavior directed at attracting the attention of a partner. It can also be done to threaten or distract predators.

Distribution
All the places where a species is located. It includes areas that the species occupies in different seasons.

Diversity
Degree to which the total number of individual organisms in an ecosystem is distributed among different species.

Echolocation
The ability to orient by emitting sounds and interpreting their echoes.

Embryo
The first stage of development of a multicellular animal or plant.

Epidermis
The outer layer of the skin.

Evolution
Gradual process of change of a species to adjust to its environment.

Exoskeleton
The external covering supporting the body, commonly found in arthropods.

Family
A category in taxonomy lower than order and higher than genus.

Fertilization
Union of male and female reproductive cells that will create a new individual.

Follicle
A small organ in the form of a sac located in skin or mucous membranes.

Fossil
Remains of various types of ancient life-forms, both plants and animals, in a rocky substrate.

Fry
Newly hatched fish whose shape resembles that of adults.

Gene
Unit of information in a chromosome; sequence of nucleotides in DNA that carries out a specific function.

Genus
A category in taxonomy that groups species together.

Gestation
The state of an embryo inside a female mammal from conception until birth.

Gizzard
Muscular stomach of a bird. It is very robust, especially in granivores, and is used to grind and soften food.

Gland
Group of cells that produce secretions, organized inside a membrane to form an organ whose function is to synthesize and excrete molecules.

Gonad
Gland that produces reproductive sex cells.

Habitat
The set of geophysical conditions in which an individual species or a community of animals or plants lives.

Herbivore
Animal that feeds exclusively on plants.

Heterocercal
Tail fin in which the spine curves upward, forming a large upper lobe.

Hibernation
The physiological state that occurs in certain mammals as an adaptation to extreme winter conditions, exhibited as a drop in body temperature and a general decrease in metabolic function.

Homeothermy
Thermoregulation characteristic of animals that maintain a constant internal temperature, regardless of external conditions.

Incubation
The act of keeping eggs warm so that the embryos inside can grow and hatch.

Invertebrate
Animal without a spinal column, such as worms and arthropods.

Keel
Ridge or fleshy border along the sides of the caudal peduncle.

Keratin
A protein rich in sulfur, the chief element of the outermost layers of mammals' epidermises, including hair, horns, nails, and hooves.

Lactation
The period in mammals' lives when they feed solely on maternal milk.

Larva
Animal in a developmental stage, after leaving the egg. It can feed itself but has not yet acquired the shape and structure of the adults of its species.

Lateral Line
Line along the sides of the fish's body consisting of a series of pores.

Lipids
Water-insoluble substances including fats, oils, waxes, steroids, glycolipids, phospholipids, and carotenes.

Mandible
Appendage just below the antennae, used to trap, hold, bite, or chew food.

Mantle
In mollusks, the outer layer of the body wall or a soft extension of it. It usually secretes a shell.

Marsupial
Mammals whose females give birth to unviable infants, which are then incubated in the ventral pouch, where the mammary glands are located.

Metabolism
The sum of all the physical and chemical transformations that occur within a cell or organism.

Metacarpus
The set of elongated bones that make up the skeleton of the anterior limbs of certain animals and of the human hand.

Metamorphosis
Abrupt transition from the larval form to the adult form.

Microorganism
Organism that can be seen only with a microscope.

Mimetism
Property of certain animals and plants to resemble living things or inanimate objects that live nearby.

Mimicry
Ability of certain organisms to modify their appearance to resemble elements of their habitat or other species.

Molars
Group of teeth that crush or grind food.

Mollusk
Invertebrate with a soft body divided into a head, foot, and visceral mass.

Molting
Removal of all or part of the outer covering of an organism; in arthropods, a periodic changing of the exoskeleton.

Morphology
Study of the form of an object.

Neuron
A differentiated cell of the nervous system capable of transmitting nerve impulses. It is composed of a receptor site, dendrites, and a transmission (or release) site—the axon, or neurite.

Nidicolous
Descriptive of a chick that depends on its parents' care after birth.

Order
Taxonomic category lower than a class and higher than a family.

Organ
Body part made of various tissues grouped into a functional unit.

Organism
Any living creature, whether single-celled or multicellular.

Ovary
Organ that produces female sex cells.

Oviduct
The duct through which the ova leave the ovary to be fertilized.

Papillae
Small conical elevations on skin or mucous membranes, especially those on the tongue used to taste.

Parasite
Organism that lives at the expense of another and typically obtains nutrients already processed by the host.

Pheromones
Chemical substances secreted by the reproductive glands of animals to attract individuals of the opposite sex.

Photophore
Mucous glands modified for the production of light, from either symbiotic phosphorescent bacteria or oxidation processes within the tissues.

Phylum
Taxonomic category lower than a kingdom and higher than a class.

Pigment
Substance that colors skin, feathers, or tissues of animals and plants.

Placenta
The spongy tissue that completely surrounds the embryo and whose function is to allow the exchange of substances through the blood.

Plankton
Group of small plants (phytoplankton) or animals (zooplankton) that live suspended in water.

Polyandry
Copulation by a female with various males during one breeding period.

Protein
Macromolecule composed of one or more chains of amino acids.

Protractile
Describes a type of reptilian tongue that can be voluntarily hurled outward in a rapid, precise movement.

Reef
Hard bank that barely reaches above the ocean surface or that lies in very shallow waters. It can be inorganic or result from the growth of coral.

Retina
The inner membrane of the eyes, where light sensations are transformed into nerve impulses.

Salinity
Measurement of the amount of common salt in water or soil.

Scales
Small bony plates that grow from the skin and overlap each other.

Scavenger
Animal that eats organic forms of life that have already died.

School
Transient grouping of fish of the same population or species, brought together by similar behavior.

Spawning
Action of producing or laying eggs.

Species
A group of individuals that recognize one another as belonging to the same reproductive unit.

Spiracle
One of the external openings of the respiratory system in terrestrial arthropods.

Substrate
The surface that constitutes an organism's habitat or life support.

Thermal
Hot air current that rises. Many birds use it to gain height effortlessly.

Thorax
In crustaceans and insects, the fused segments located between the head and the abdomen to which the legs are attached.

Tissue
Group of identical cells that carry out a common function.

Trachea
In insects and some other terrestrial arthropods, the system of air conduits covered with chitin.

Tundra
Vast treeless plains in Arctic regions.

Vertebrates
Animals that have a spinal column, such as birds, fish, reptiles, amphibians, and mammals.

Viviparous
Refers to animals in which the embryonic development of offspring occurs inside the mother's body and the offspring emerge as viable young.

Weaning
The process by which a mammal ceases to receive maternal milk as its subsistence.

INDEX

A

alligator, 47
  American, 42
amphibians, 6–7, 60–63
anglerfish, humpback 59
ants, 74–75
  cleaning with, in birds, 31
aposematism, 72
aquatic birds, 5, 36
arachnids, 68–69
assassin bug, 77
Atlantic football fish, 59

B

barnacles, 66
bats, 4–5, 26–27
bear, grizzly, 9
beetles, 72, 73
  Japanese rhinoceros, 71
bills, 5, 28, 36, 37, 38, 41
birds, 5, 9, 28–41
  flightless, 34–35
  freshwater, 36–37
  of prey, 5, 38–39
birdsong, 40
bivalves, 65
boa constrictor, 43, 48, 49
bradycardia, 23
broadbills, 40, 41
butterflies, 76
buzzards, 39

C

caecilian, ringed, 61
caiman, 42, 47
camouflage, 44, 76
carnivores, 16
cartilaginous fish, 51
cassowary, 34, 35
catfish, upside-down, 52
centipede, 71
cephalopods, 65
cetaceans, 9, 22–25
chameleon, 44
cheetah, 14–15
chelonians, 43
chickens, 33, 35
chimpanzees, 4–5, 8
chipmunk, 8
Choanichthyes, 51
cicadas, 73
cobra, King, 49
coelacanth, 51
communication, 5
  underwater, 24–25
condors, 39
conservation, 7
copepoda, 67
cows, 4, 18–19
crab, 66
  European green, 67
  Japanese spider, 66

crocodile, 5, 6, 42, 46–47
crustaceans, 66–67
curlew, stone, 37
cuttlefish, common, 65

D

deer, 18
divers, 37
dodo, 34
dogs, 4, 11, 12–13, 14
dolphins, 4–5, 50
  bottlenose, 8, 24–25
domestication, 4
dragonfish, 59
dragonfly, 70
ducks, 36
dust bath, 31

E

eagle owl, 7
eagles, 39
  bald, 38
  martial, 21
echidna, short-beaked, 11
echolocation, 25
ectothermy, 43
eggs, 6
  birds, 32–33
  reptiles, 42
electricity, 54
elephant, 11
emu, 34
evolution, 76–77
extinction, 7
eyes, 8
  compound, 70
  in birds of prey, 38, 39

F

falcon, 38, 39
fanfin seadevil, 58
fangtooth, 58
feathers, 30–31
fish, 6, 50–59
  abyssal, 58–59
fleas, 68
flight, 26–27, 28
  insect, 72–73
flightless birds, 5
frogs, 60, 61, 62, 63
fumarole, 59
furcula (collarbone), 28

G

gastropods, 64
geckos, 44
geese, 36
gharial, 46
gibbons, 11
gila monster, 45
gills, 50
  in tadpoles, 62

giraffes, 11
goose, white-fronted, 36
gorilla, 8, 9
goshawk, 38, 39
grebe, 37

H

hagfish, 51
hawks, 38, 39
heloderma, 45
herbivores, 18–19
heron, imperial, 31
herring, 53
hibernation, 9, 27
homeothermy, 9
horses, 4, 14
humans, 4, 7, 8, 9, 14
hummingbird, 5, 28, 32, 40
hunting, 17
hydrostatic pressure, 59

IJK

ibis, white, 37
iguana, common, 45
illuminated netdevil, 59
insects, 70–75
jackal, black-backed, 20
Jaws, 55
keratin, 31
kingfisher, 36, 37
kites, 39
kiwi, 5, 33, 34, 35
koala, 11

L

lactation, 10, 11
ladybug, 72–73
lamprey, 51
lions, 11, 16–17
lizards, 5, 14, 43, 44–45
lure organs, 58
lyrebirds, 40

M

mackerel, Atlantic, 50
mammals, 4, 8–27
  characteristics, 8
  life cycle, 10–11
mantis, thistle, 77
Maori hen, 33
Mariana Trench, 59
marsupials, 11
meerkat, 20–21
Mesozoic era, 42
metamorphosis, 62–63, 74
migration, 5
  in birds, 41
  in salmon, 56–57
millipedes, 71
mimetism, 77
mites, 68
mollusks, 64–65

monotremes, 11
mussel, green, 65
myriapods, 70, 71

N

nautilus, 65
newts, 61

O

Oceania, 35
octopus, 65
omasum, 19
ostrich, 5, 32, 34–35
ovenbirds, 40, 41
ovule, 32
owl, 76
  Eurasian eagle, 38
owl pellets 38

P

passerines, 40–41
pelican, 37
penguins, 5, 34
perching, 29, 41
pheasant, 35
pigs, 4
plankton, 67
platypus, 11
play, 24
powder down, 31
prawns, 67
preening, 31
primates, 9
prosobranchia, 64
pythons, 6, 48

R

rabbit, eastern cottontail, 10
ram ventilation, 50
ratites, 35
rattlesnake, 49
raven, 40
ray, 51
reptiles, 5–6, 42–49
rhea, 5, 34, 35
rumination, 18–19
running, 14

S

sailfish, 52
salamander, tiger, 61
salmon, Pacific red, 56–57
scallop, 65
scorpions, 68
sea angel, 64
sea lice, 66, 67
sea slugs, 64
seals, 4–5, 50
senses, 12–13
shark, 51
  great white, 52, 54–55

sheep, 4, 18
shoebill, 37
shrimp, 67
skinks, 42, 44
sloth, three-toed, 15
slugs, 64
smell, 13
  in sharks, 54
snails, 64–65
snakes, 5, 6, 43, 48–49
sonar, 26
songbirds, 40
sparrow, 32
spermaceti, 22, 23
spiders, 68, 69
squamata, 43
squid, giant, 64
squirrel, Siberian flying, 14–15
stick insect, Australian, 77
storks, 36, 37
swallows, 40, 41
swans, 31, 36
  black-necked, 36
sweat glands, 8
swimming, in ducks, 36
  in fish, 52–53
syrinx, 40, 41

T

tadpoles, 62–63
taste, 13
teeth, 18
  carnivore, 16
  crocodile, 47
  fish, 58
  herbivore, 18
  mammal, 8
  shark, 55
  whale, 22
ticks, 68
toads, 60, 61
tortoise, Hermann's, 43
tube worms, 59
turkey, 35
turtles, 5, 43

V

vibrissae, 31
viperfish, Sloane's, 58
vipers, 49
  gaboon, 49
vultures, 39

W

wading birds, 37
wallabies, 11
warm-bloodedness, 27
whales, 10, 50
  sperm, 22–23
wings, bat, 27
  birds, 28
wood louse, 66